CW01304997

The Complete Book of Fruit Carving

Decorate your table for any special occasion

Rie Yamada

Contents

Preface / 5

Basic Tools / 13
Carving Tools / 14
Using Carving Knives / 16

Basic Techniques / 17
Tips for Getting Started / 18
"レ" Shape / 19
"V" Shape / 20
Eye-Like Shape / 21
Waterdrop Shape / 22
Conical Shape / 23
Square Lattice Shape / 24

Carving Vegetables and Fruits / 25
Apple / 26
Watermelon / 28
Carrot / 30
Cherry Radish / 30
Turnip or a White Radish / 31
Orange, Grapefruit, and Yuzu / 32
Cucumber / 33
Melon / 33
Pumpkin / 34
Strawberry / 34
Colored Pepper / 35
Zucchini / 35

Art Exhibition—Decorative Flowers / 36

Japanese New Year / 37
Fashionable Japanese-Style Displays for New Year's Celebration / 38
Happy New Year / 40
Plum Blossom 1 / 42
Plum Blossom 2 / 43
Plum Blossom 3 / 44
Plum Blossom 4 / 46
Bamboo / 47
Pine / 48
Turnip Shuttlecock Board / 49
Basket (with Handle) / 50
Basket (without Handle) / 52
Turnip Fan 1 / 54
Turnip Fan 2 / 55
Turnip Crane / 56
Turnip Turtle / 58
Yuzu Jar (with Lid) / 60
Yuzu Jar (without Lid) / 64

Practical Tips: Thai Knife Maintenance / 66

Hinamatsuri (Girl's Day in Japan) / 67
Spring Party / 68
Strawberry Tulips / 70
Colored Pepper Tulips / 72
Carrot Butterfly / 74
Cucumber Leaf 1, 2, and 3 / 76
Orange Basket / 82
Melon Bowl / 84

Halloween / 89

Pumpkin Toy Box / 90
Carrot Jack-O'-Lantern / 92
Alternative Jack-O'-Lanterns / 94
Halloween Pumpkin Lantern / 96
Flower Carved Lantern / 102
Heart Carved Lantern / 103
Cross Carved Lantern / 104
Triangle Carved Lantern / 105
Fireworks Carved Lantern / 106

Christmas / 107

Apple Christmas Tree / 108
Forest Christmas / 110
Fireworks / 112
Flowers and Diamonds / 114
Hearts and Waterdrops / 117
Hearts and Flowers 1 / 120
Hearts and Flowers 2 / 123
Oriental Style / 126
Floral Design Candlestick / 131

Practical Tips: Preserving Apple Works / 134

Birthday / 135

Watermelon Birthday Party / 136
Happy Birthday Lettering / 138
Lined Hearts / 143
Watermelon Cake / 144
Watermelon Bowl / 148
Various Cherry Radish Works / 151
Zucchini Boat-Shaped Plate / 155
Colored Pepper Dish / 156

Art Exhibition—The Charm of Carving / 158
Art Exhibition—Ingenious Seasonal Design / 158

Wedding / 159

The Beauty of Blessing / 160
Rose Welcome Decoration / 162
Big Rose / 164
Happy Wedding Watermelon / 174
Initials of First Names / 178
A Welcome Watermelon / 182
Lettering the Couple's Names / 185
Bride Silhouette / 188
Fan Theme / 194

Rie and Hitomi's Art Exhibition / 199

Art Exhibition—Watermelon Pieces / 200
Art Exhibition—Soap Carvings / 204

4

Preface

All you need is a knife to begin fruit carving!

It is said that fruit carving originated in the Thai court. To lay out a decorative, gorgeous table, the chef started carving vegetables and fruits. There are many classes for fruit carving enthusiasts in Thailand, and new techniques and designs continue to emerge.

This book presents authentic carving techniques from Thailand and projects to be enjoyed through all seasons. It includes basics that beginners need to master as well as more advanced projects, allowing readers to acquire the necessary techniques step by step.

If you imagine the surprised looks on the faces of your family and friends when they see you present a sculpture made with your own hands, the entire carving process can be a wonderful time! Experience this refreshing feeling together with the people you love the most, enjoy a great sense of accomplishment, and give them the most beautiful works.

I hope this book will bring color to your life as well as a smile to your face.

Rie Yamada

New Year's Day

Hinamatsuri (Girl's Day in Japan on March 3rd)

Halloween

Christmas

Birthday

Wedding

12

basic tools

Tools necessary for carving, and how to use a carving knife.

13

basic tools

Carving tools

Thai knife

There are beautiful patterns on the handle and the case of the knife. The blade is thinner than those of ordinary carving knives. Because it has a curved edge, it is recommended for skilled users. The tip of the blade can be used to underline. A wide range of Thai knives with various blade lengths and thicknesses are available online. Search the internet by "Thai carving knife" or "carving knife."

Carving knife

The blade of a carving knife is very thin, and it carves a very thin line, so it is suitable for carving the details of delicate designs as though they are being painted. Although the blade is quite thin, it does not bend easily, and it does not waver when cutting curves or cutting vigorously. This makes it quite convenient for shaping. To purchase a carving knife, you can go to a hand tool shop or order online.

Fruit knife

A fruit knife can be used for the initial cutting and rough shaping of the fruit being used. For reasons of safety, it is better to select a fruit knife that has a strong blade, a comfortable handle with a blade that does not loosen from the handle so that the blade does not sway when being used.

Molds

Molds are used for making preliminary shapes. There are many types of molds, such as those of plum blossoms and pine trees, which can be used for many projects. When using a mold, place the fruit on the table and press the mold down from directly above it.

Melon baller

A melon baller is used for removing pits from fruit. Insert the round scoop on the front end of the melon baller into the pulp of a fruit, such as a watermelon or melon, and spin it out to get a perfect ball.

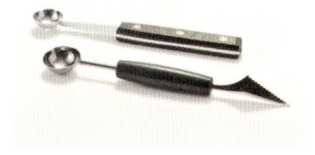

basic tools

Using carving knives

Holding the knife like a pen
When making a sculpture, the most basic work consists of cutting, removing material, and drawing details, all of which have to be completed through "pen-style holding." During the carving process, the knife can be stabilized by placing the middle finger on the side of the blade. The knife should be held with the fingers positioned as in the picture.

Gripping the knife
This method of cutting is suitable for carving large areas. Hold the knife handle tightly, place the thumb on the area of the blade circled with an "○" in the picture, and apply a little force. Be careful not to place the other hand where the blade will be moving.

Using the ring finger as a fulcrum
When carving vegetables or fruits, the key is to support the carving hand using the ring finger as a fulcrum to prevent the hand from shaking and to make it easier to adjust the distance between the knife and the fruit, making the carving process easier.

basic techniques
Common styling and carving steps.

Tips for Getting Started

Do you want to carve a masterpiece?
The biggest secret is mastering the basic skills.

The projects in this book are all combinations and applications of basic carving techniques. It is important to practice these basic techniques repeatedly and master the use of the carving knife. For example, in "レ"-shaped carving, the first cut should be made vertically, and the second cut should be inclined by tilting the knife next to the line drawn by making the first cut. If the second cut was deeper than the first one by even only a few millimeters, it would affect the beauty of the incision.

In waterdrop-shaped and conical-shaped carvings, the fruit and the knife must be rotated simultaneously, but if the incision does not match the beauty of the whole work would be diminished.

To produce an outstanding piece of work, first practice the basics. It is a must to practice carving techniques with different widths and depths.

basic techniques

"レ" shape

Difficulty ● ○ ○ ○ ○

1 Insert the blade vertically 5mm deep, then carve.

2 Draw a heart-shaped outline.

3 Tilt the knife 45 degrees and carve along the inside of the first outline.

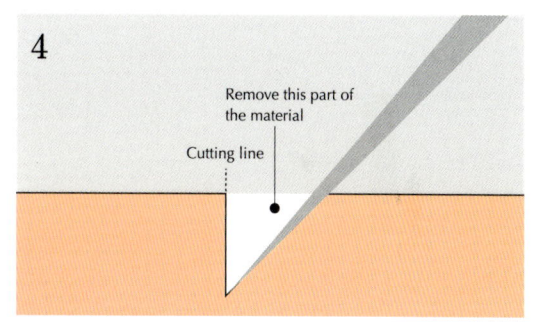

4 Step 3 should look like this.

Remove this part of the material
Cutting line

5 Because the first incision is made vertically, and the second made at a 45 degree, the final result is a "レ"-shaped cut.

6 The final result when the step is repeated.

19

basic techniques
"V" shape

Difficulty | ● ○ ○ ○ ○

1

Carve at a 45 degree angle along the three lines in the picture.

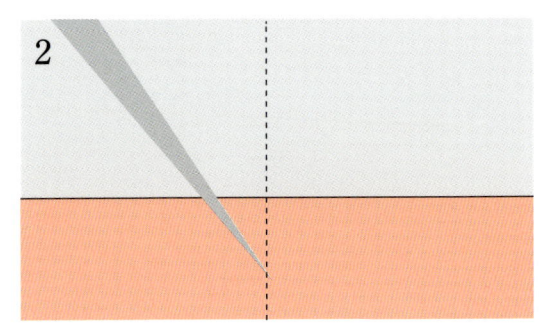

2

Step 1 should look like this.

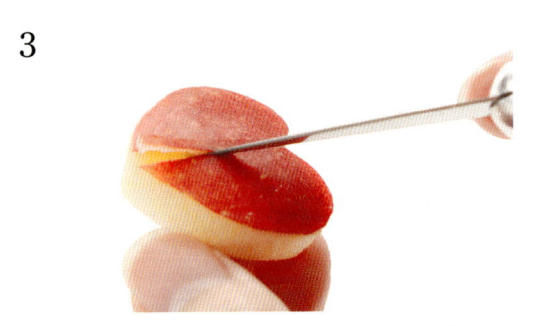

3

Cut from the opposite direction at a 45 degree angle, meeting the groove cut in step 1.

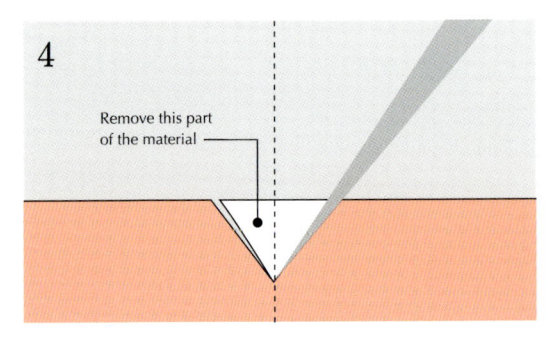

4

Remove this part of the material

Step 3 should look like this.

5

The groove that is cut out makes a "V" shape.

6

This is the result when the step is repeated.

basic techniques
Eye-like shape

Difficulty ●● ○ ○ ○

1

Cut at a 45 degree angle, gently moving the blade from left to right to make a semicircle.

2

Turn the apple upside down, cutting at a 45 degree angle to cut out another semicircle that connects with the semicircle cut in step 1.

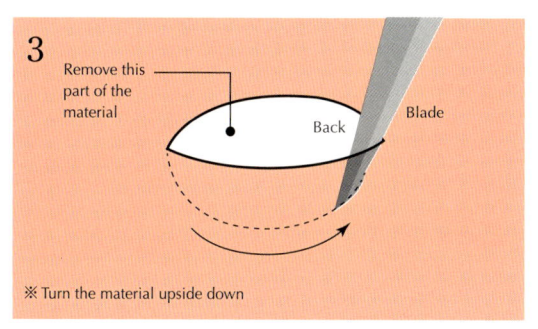

3

Remove this part of the material
Back
Blade
※ Turn the material upside down

Step 2 should look like this.

4

Because it is shaped like an eye, it is called an eye-like shape.

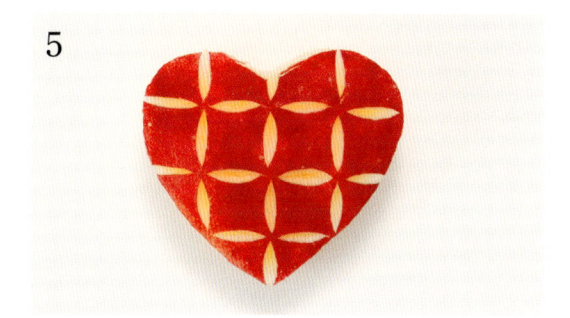

5

This is the result when the process is repeated vertically and horizontally.

21

basic techniques

Waterdrop shape

Difficulty ● ● ● ○ ○

1

Tilt the knife to the left-hand side, and fix the blade to cut out a "∟" shape. With the fixed blade as the starting point, rotate the knife to carve a "U"-shape. As shown in the picture, the knife is tilted to the right.

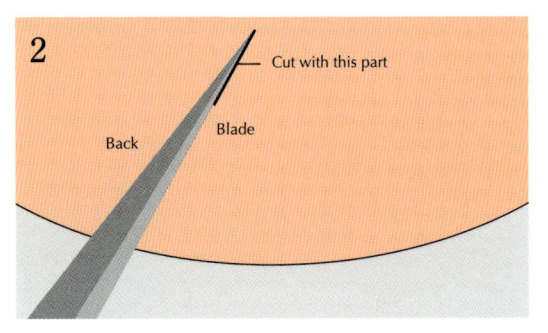

2

Cut with this part
Back   Blade

Step 1 should look like this.

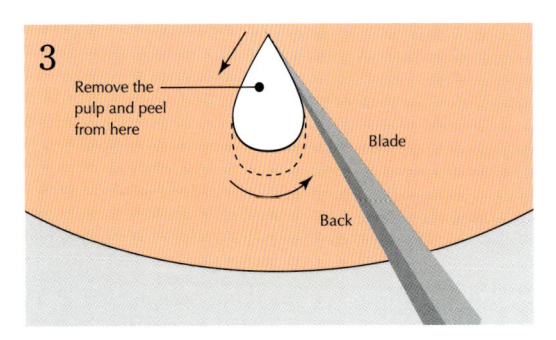

3

Remove the pulp and peel from here
Blade
Back

Step 1 should look like this.

4

Maintain the same angle, and finally, remove the peel and pulp inside the outline of the waterdroplets.

5

Repeat the process to complete the design.

basic techniques

Conical shape

Difficulty ● ● ● ● ○

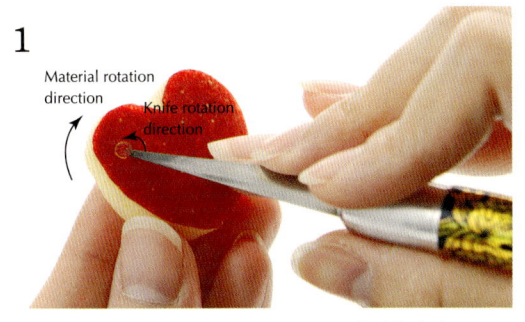

1

Cut by tilting the knife 45 degrees with the blade being fixed. Rotate the knife counterclockwise and the material clockwise.

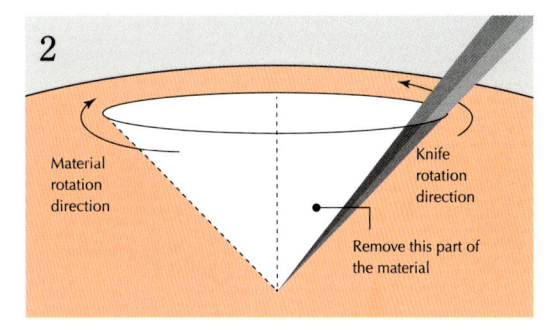

2

This shows how to move the knife in step 1.

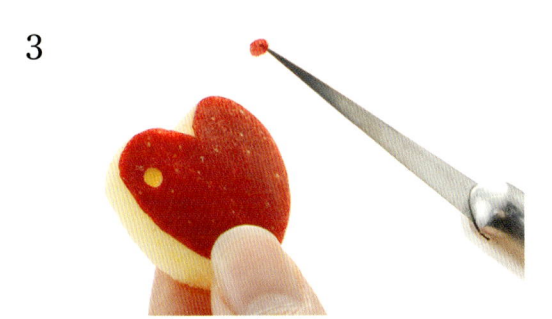

3

The knife should rotate one full circle, with the starting point coinciding with the ending point. Then, remove the peel in the middle. A conical shape is carved out.

4

Repeat the process to complete the design.

23

basic techniques

Square lattice shape

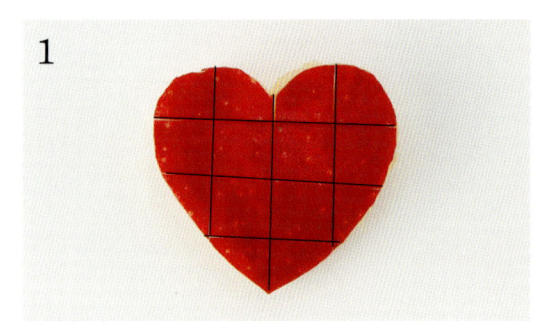

Difficulty ● ● ● ● ○

1

Carve horizontal and vertical lines 5mm deep.

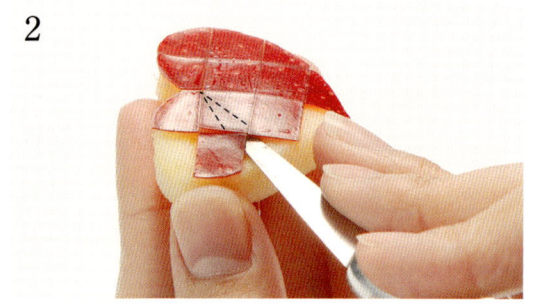

2

When peeling the inner square, the carving knife should be inserted horizontally from one corner of the square. Then, gently remove the peel.

3

The peel in one square of the grid is removed.

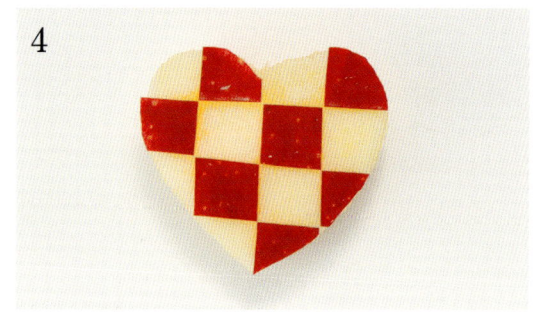

4

Every other square is peeled, and the lattice shape is carved.

carving vegetables and fruits

Vegetables and fruits used in the sculptures in this book.

25

carving vegetables and fruits
Apple

Key tips
When using an apple for carving, try to select an apple of dark red to make full use of the contrast between the red of the surface and the white of the pulp. Try also to use an apple with a full round shape and stable base. Because apple peels are very thin, if too much force is applied the carved line can become rickety and unseemly. Particular care is needed when making delicate designs with parts of the peel left. Pay attention to the movement of the blade while piercing and slicing.

Carving works made from apples

Fireworks
Difficulty / ●●○○○
See p. 112

Flowers and diamonds
Difficulty / ●●○○○
See p. 114

Hearts and waterdrops
Difficulty / ●●●○○
See p. 117

Hearts and flowers 1
Difficulty / ●●●●○
See p. 120

Hearts and flowers 2
Difficulty / ●●●●○
See p. 123

Oriental style
Difficulty / ●●●●●
See p. 126

Pattern candlestick
Difficulty / ●●●●●
See p. 131

Lined hearts
Difficulty / ●○○○○
See p. 143

Displaying of apple works

Use apples to build a Christmas tree and place it against a white background with stylish golden accessories.

Place apples in containers with height, together with a Christmas wreath. The small gift boxes add fun to the Christmas spirit.

The bright red of apples is eye-catching when displayed against a silver-white background. The candlelight that shimmers above the intricate designs turns any scene into one of quite sophistication.

27

carving vegetables and fruits

Watermelon

Key tips

When using watermelons for carving, it is important to choose mature ones. The pulp of underripe watermelons are not firm, and large cracks may appear while carving. Tap the watermelon lightly, and if the sound vibrates well, the fruit is suited for carving. If the sound is dull, it indicates a over-ripe fruit, which is not suitable for fine carving. Watermelon peels are hard, so it is important to carve with dynamic movements, piercing slightly and pulling gently while cutting forward.

The most suitable watermelon cultivar is "Luna Piena" from Japan. Although watermelons cannot usually be found in winter, the "Luna Piena" cultivar is available in all seasons. This kind of watermelon does not crack easily when being carved because it cannot be harvested unless it is mature, and in comparison with other cultivars the peel is relatively soft. In addition, the color of the pulp is quite beautiful so it is highly recommended.

Carving works made from watermelons

Happy birthday lettering
Difficulty / ●●●●●
See p. 138

Watermelon cake
Difficulty / ●●●○○
See p. 144

Watermelon bowl
Difficulty / ●○○○○
See p. 148

Big rose
Difficulty / ●●●●○
See p. 164

Wedding blessing watermelon
Difficulty / ●●●●●
See p. 174

Initials of first names
Difficulty / ●●●●●
See p. 178

A welcome watermelon
Difficulty / ●●●●●
See p. 182

Lettering of a couple's names
Difficulty / ●●●●●
See p. 185

Bride silhouette
Difficulty / ●●●●○
See p. 188

Fan theme
Difficulty / ●●●●●
See p. 194

Displaying of watermelon works

Each watermelon is a self-standing piece of art. This display which makes full use of height and depth is perfect for decorating the reception area of a wedding.

Two exquisite watermelons designed with rose and fan motifs. They can be placed in the corner of a majestic church to create a fabulous wedding scene.

This cake design is colorful and best suited for celebrating birthdays. It is even more elegant when placed on a lace place mat.

carving vegetables and fruits

Carrot

Key tips

If the carrots are not thoroughly peeled, they will turn black after a while. Therefore, peel them thoroughly beforehand. To prevent the carrots from wilting and becoming difficult to carve, sprinkle some water on them to keep them fresh. If bright colors are looked for in a piece, kintoki red carrots are recommended. Carrots are easy to carve, so practice on them before moving on to larger, more difficult projects.

Carving works made from carrots

Plum blossoms 1
Difficulty / ●○○○○
See p. 42

Plum blossoms 2
Difficulty / ●○○○○
See p. 43

Plum blossoms 3
Difficulty / ●○○○○
See p. 44

Plum blossoms 4
Difficulty / ●○○○○
See p. 46

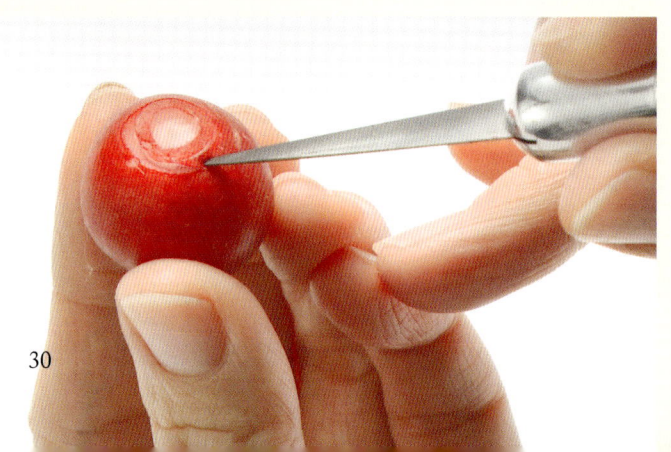

Bamboo
Difficulty / ●○○○○
See p. 47

Pine
Difficulty / ●○○○○
See p. 48

Butterfly
Difficulty / ●○○○○
See p. 74

Carrot jack-o'-lantern
Difficulty / ●●○○○
See p. 92

carving vegetables and fruits

Cherry radish

Key tips

The cherry radish's skin and pulp are soft and suitable for carving. However, they are small in size so it is best to practice on carrots and cucumbers before starting on them. After the work is completed, they should be soaked in water to keep fresh, but be careful not to soak them too long or the skin may begin to peel.

carving vegetables and fruits

Turnip or white radish

Key tips

Although the water content and hardness of the turnip (commonly known as kohlrabi) and the white radish are different, they can both be used to make white-colored decorations. Because it is difficult to distinguish cuts made on white material, the first cut may not be visible, making it difficult to balance the second cut with it. The appearance of the incision will affect the overall look of the work, so it is necessary to be careful.

Carving works made from turnips

Turnip shuttlecock board
Difficulty / ●○○○○
See p. 49

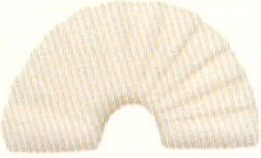

Turnip fan 1
Difficulty / ●○○○○
See p. 54

Turnip fan 2
Difficulty / ●○○○○
See p. 55

Turnip crane
Difficulty / ●●●○○
See p. 56

Turnip turtle
Difficulty / ●●●○○
See p. 58

Carving works made from cherry radishs

Cherry radish jack-o'-lantern
Difficulty / ●○○○○
See p. 95

Cherry radish 1
Difficulty / ●●○○○
See p. 151

Cherry radish 2
Difficulty / ●●○○○
See p. 152

Cherry radish 3
Difficulty / ●●○○○
See p. 152

Cherry radish 4
Difficulty / ●●○○○
See p. 153

Cherry radish 5
Difficulty / ●●○○○
See p. 153

Cherry radish 6
Difficulty / ●●○○○
See p. 154

carving vegetables and fruits

Orange, grapefruit and yuzu

Key tips
It is mainly the peel that is used for carving, so it is important to remove the pulp properly, particularly the white fiber (tangerine pith) on the inside of the peel. If too much remains, it will have an impact on the carving process and final work. Therefore, it is necessary to spend time preparing.

Carving works made from oranges, grapefruits and yuzu

Yuzu jar (with lid)
Difficulty / ●●○○○
See p. 60

Yuzu jar (without lid)
Difficulty / ●●○○○
See p. 64

Orange basket
Difficulty / ●○○○○
See p. 82

Flower carved lantern
Difficulty / ●●○○○
See p. 102

Heart carved lantern
Difficulty / ●●○○○
See p. 103

Cross carved lantern
Difficulty / ●●○○○
See p. 104

Triangle carved lantern
Difficulty / ●●○○○
See p. 105

Fireworks carved lantern
Difficulty / ●●○○○
See p. 106

Displaying of orange, grapefruit and yuzu works

This is a delicate and fashionable yuzu jar decorated colorfully with the festival dish.
 * A traditional Japanese New Year's dish.

Adorable orange baskets tied with ribbons. Its freshness goes well with Hinamatsuri (Girl's Day in Japan) as well as other parties.

Orange or grape fruit lanterns carved with diverse patterns are placed together to create an artistic array of lights and shadows.

carving vegetables and fruits
Cucumber

Key tips
Cucumbers with a lot of bumps on the surface are difficult to carve. Try to select the relatively smooth type. Since thin cucumbers are not suitable for contouring, it's better to choose thick ones, particularly when carving leaves. Beginners should practice on cucumbers first.

Cucumber works

Basket (with handle)
Difficulty / ●○○○○
See p. 50

Basket (without handle)
Difficulty / ●○○○○
See p. 52

Cucumber leaf 1, 2 and 3
Difficulty / ●○○○○
See p. 76

carving vegetables and fruits
Melon

Key tips
Fully ripe melons are not suitable for carving. Select a melon that is hard at the bottom and has no fragrance. Although netted melons can be used for carving, for some projects it is better to select un-netted ones to enhance the design. Honeydew melons without netlike markings on the skin are recommended.

Melon works

Melon bowl
Difficulty / ●●●●○
See p. 84

carving vegetables and fruits
Pumpkin

Key tips
While edible pumpkins are not suitable for carving, Halloween pumpkins are fitting because of their hollowness and soft skin. The seeds inside the pumpkin should be cleaned out thoroughly before carving; otherwise, it will cause the pumpkin to rot faster.

Pumpkin works

Halloween pumpkin lantern
Difficulty / ●●○○○
See p. 96

carving vegetables and fruits
Strawberry

Key tips
Ripe strawberries are not suitable for carving because they are too soft to cut sharp lines, so harder strawberries should be chosen. In addition, the color and size of strawberries are generally uneven, so it is preferable to select strawberries of a uniform shape and color.

Strawberry works

Strawberry tulip
Difficulty / ●●○○○
See p. 70

carving vegetables and fruits
Colored pepper

Key tips
Colored peppers are soft and easy to work on. However, if they are withered it is difficult to carve sharp lines on them, so soak them in water for a while to make them fresh. They are very colorful, and if prepared properly the seeds can also be used as part of the artwork.

Colored pepper works

Colored pepper tulip
Difficulty / ●○○○○
See p. 72

Colored pepper dish
Difficulty / ●○○○○
See p. 156

carving vegetables and fruits
Zucchini

Key tips
As with cucumbers, zucchinis can also be used to carve leaves. However, this time they are used to make boat-shaped plates to display cherry radishes on. While the white parts of cucumbers cannot be used for carving because their seeds are so conspicuous, zucchini seeds are less visible so designs can be made on the white flesh to add flavor to the entire work.

Zucchini works

Zucchini boat-shaped plate
Difficulty / ●○○○○
See p. 155

art exhibition

Decorative flowers

Dahlias made with pumpkins
Japanese pumpkins are often avoided because they are hard, but after they are warmed slightly in the microwave, they become soft and easy to carve. Carved into a flower, they are surprisingly durable, and perfect for adding color to the table.

A rose basket made with carrots
Carve flowers out of carrots and insert them into baskets that are also made from vegetables to complete a wonderful floral arrangement. If red colored peppers are used, remove a part of it and insert a flower project into the incision. Such works look stunning when displayed at an entrance, perfect for welcoming even the most unexpected of guests.

Carving leaves with an apple
It is often cucumbers, white radishes and carrots that are used for carving leaves, but using the red and white contrast of apples for leaves is recommended as well.

Plumeria made with a white radish
The center of the flower is rendered with yellow food coloring to create life-like flowers. Decorate a salad plate with these flowers, together with leaves made from cucumbers.

Japanese New Year

A Japanese-style arrangement that signifies happiness and adds color and flavor to New Year's dishes.

Japanese New Year

Fashionable Japanese-style displays for New Year's celebration

Red cranes and white turtles, both symbols of long life, lavishly displayed on gold plates. The elegant cloth mat and black background is combined for a modern-Japanese chic look.

Vegetables and fruits to be used

Carrots, turnips, red radishes and cucumbers

Key tips

Crane
Red and white, colors of good omen, are used in Japanese festivities. The "red" is taken from the crane carved from red radish. The pale red of the radishes are beautiful, and they are large and thick enough to cut into size to match the turnip or white radish.

Turtle
As with the crane, the turtle is characterized by its round form. The head, feet, shell, and tail of the turtle should be molded to be as round as possible, and the straight lines on the shell surface should be engraved as clearly as possible. Although small, it is a very artistic piece of work.

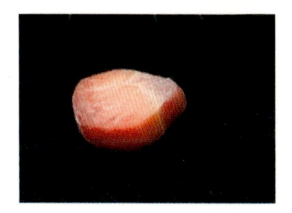

Plum blossoms
Plum blossoms are carved from carrots. Cut them in various thicknesses and sizes to add movement to the display. Shave thin slices of petal and scatter them across the black scenery for added effect.

Ensemble
New Year's displays are full of traditional Japanese elements. To make the display a little more modern, choose a black display and a chic cloth mat. Use deep colors for the tableware to keep the tone calm. The crane and the turtle, the center elements, should be placed on gold plates to make them stand out.

Japanese New Year

Happy New Year

Celebrate the beginning of a new year with traditional New Year motifs and decorations. Use *washi* and Japanese *chirimen* crepe fabric and make the scene especially Japanese.

Vegetables and fruits to be used

Carrots, turnips, cucumbers and yuzu

Key tips

Upper part

A bright, warm colored paper is selected to reflect the New Year sunrise. The artwork is displayed on a black tray in the center. A yuzu bowl filled with festive food is placed at the top, with green cucumbers at its side to emulate the first sun rising from the mountains.

Lower part

The foot of the mountain is an assortment of reds and whites. Cranes, turtles, pines, bamboos, plums, shuttlecock boards and fans are all fundamental to the Japanese New Year. Arrange them dynamically so that the overall effect is lively and festive.

Vegetables and fruits to be used
Carrots

Key tips
The round form of the plum blossoms are very cute, and placed all together, they create an wondrous effect. The details on each plum are different, and in this book four designs are introduced. When these are mastered, use them to try some original designs as well.

Vegetables and fruits to be used
Cucumbers

Key tips
Black beans play an important role in Japanese New Year's dishes. Place them in little baskets carved from cucumbers for a display of elegance. Since they are dark in color, arrange them on a white plate in front of red Japanese patterns to make their colors vibrant.

Japanese New Year

Plum blossoms 1

Cut angles outwardly from the center of the flower to make it three-dimensional.

Difficulty ● ○ ○ ○ ○

1

Cut the carrots into round slices that are 1cm thick, and make the shape of plum blossoms with the mold.

2

Starting at the center of the flower, cut out five lines, 5mm deep, between the petals.

3

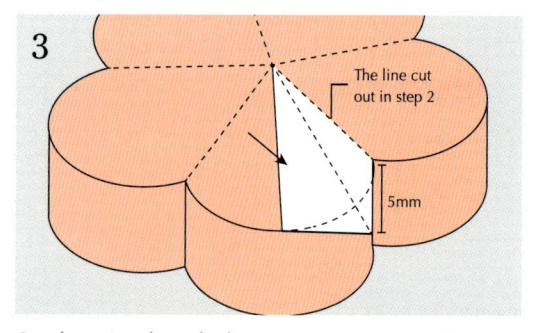

The line cut out in step 2

5mm

Cut slantwise along the line cut out in step 2, and remove the excess material.

4

Do the same for the remaining four lines, following step 3.

42

Japanese New Year

Plum blossoms 2

Master the basic skill of "レ" shape carving with this project that highlights the petals.

Difficulty ● ○ ○ ○ ○

1

Cut the carrots into round slices that are 1cm thick, and make the shape of plum blossoms with the mold.

2

Starting at the center of the flower, cut out five lines, 5mm deep, between the petals.

3

Cut a "レ"-shaped groove from each side of the lines carved in step 2 and remove the excess material.

4

Do the same for the remaining four lines, following step 3.

43

Japanese New Year

Plum blossoms 3

Create a cute plum shape using the basic carving technique of waterdrop shape.

Difficulty ● ○ ○ ○ ○

1

Cut the carrots into round slices 1cm thick, and make the shape of plum blossoms with the mold.

2

Starting at the center of the flower, cut out five lines, 5mm deep, between the petals.

3

Cut a "レ"-shaped groove from each side of the lines carved in step 2 and remove the excess material.

4

Repeat step 3 for the remaining four lines.

5

Around the center of the flower, press with the waterdrop-shaped mold to create a stamen.

6

Repeat step 5 for the remaining four positions.

7

Check each petal for uneven corners, and trim them to make them smooth and polished. A lovely plum is completed.

45

Japanese New Year

Plum blossoms 4

The center of the flower is a delicate and fine conical shape.

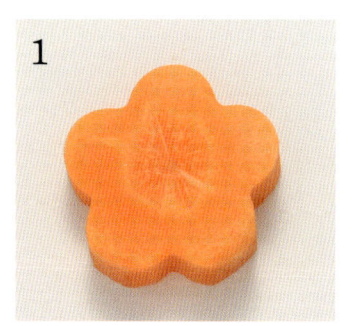

Difficulty ● ○ ○ ○ ○

1
Cut the carrots into round slices 1cm thick, and make the shape of plum blossoms with the mold.

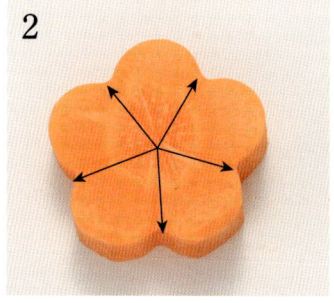

2
Starting at the center of the flower, cut out five lines, 5mm deep, between the petals.

3
Cut a "レ"-shaped groove from each side of the lines carved in step 2 and remove the excess material.

4
Repeat step 3 for the remaining four lines.

5
The flower's center is pressed with a conical mold. Cut the "V" shape in the direction from the middle of the petals to the center of the flower, and remove the excess material. Check each petal for uneven corners, and trim them to make them smooth and polished. That completes an exquisite plum blossom.

Japanese New Year

Bamboo

The waterdrop-shaped carving makes bamboo leaves more vivid.

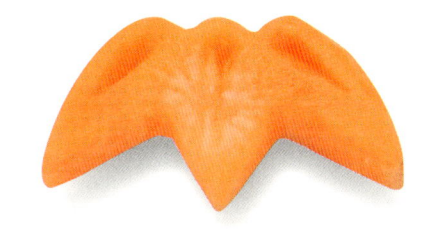

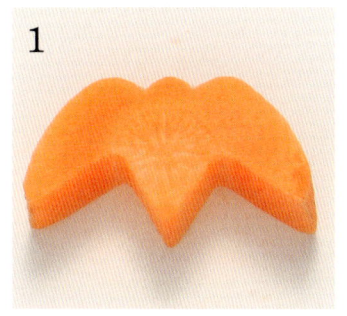

Difficulty ● ○ ○ ○ ○

1 Cut the carrots into round slices 1cm thick, and make the shape of a bamboo leaf with the mold.

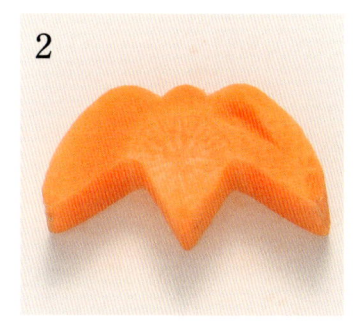

2 Carve the waterdrop shape near the root of the leaf.

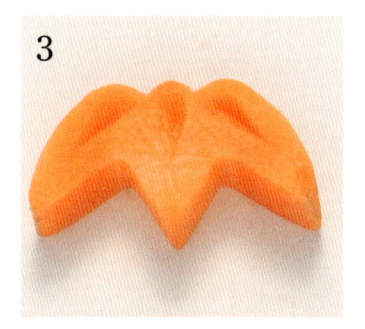

3 Repeat step 2 for the remaining two bamboo leaves.

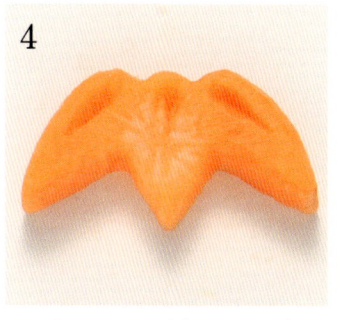

4 Trim the corners of the surrounding area to make them smooth and polished. The bamboo leaves are completed.

Japanese New Year

Pine

"レ" and "V" shapes give character to this simple shape.

Difficulty | ● ○ ○ ○ ○

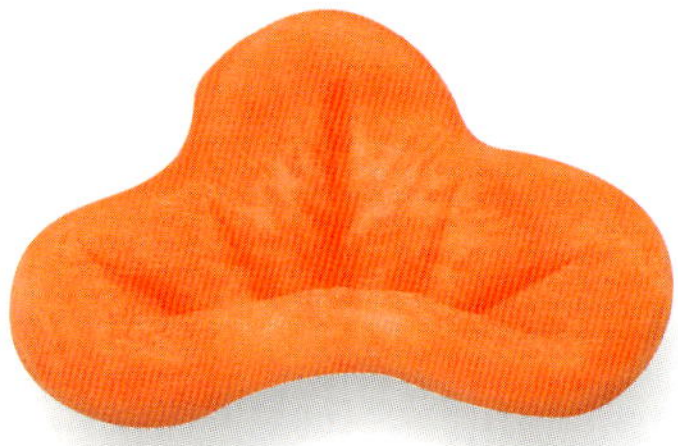

1 Cut carrots into round slices 1cm thick, and make the shape of pine tree with the mold.

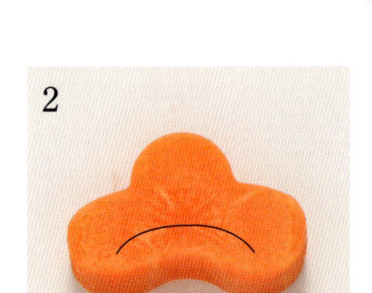

2 Carve an arc at the bottom using the line in the picture as reference.

3 Cut out a "レ"-shaped groove above the arc, and remove the excess material.

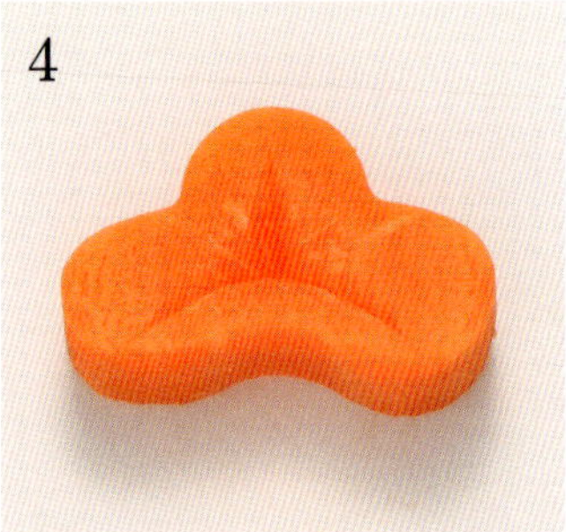

4 Cut out a relatively long "V"-shaped groove right in the middle of the arc and remove the excess material.

5 Repeat step 4 for the remaining four positions. Note that the two grooves in the middle should be a bit shorter so that the model looks more like a pine tree.

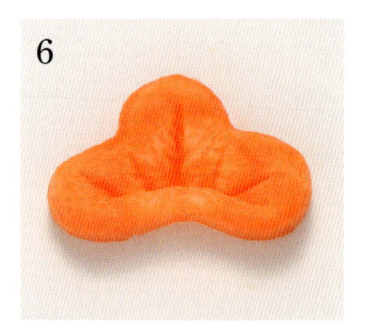

6 Trim the corners of the surrounding area to make it smooth and polished.

Japanese New Year

Turnip shuttlecock board

The red shuttlecock design made from carrots against the white turnip board, a design using the two main colors of New Year.

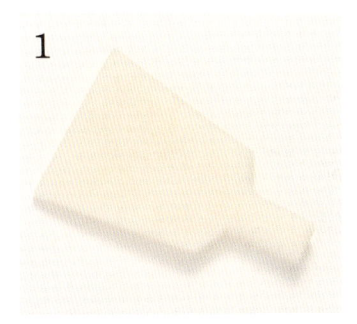

Difficulty ● ○ ○ ○ ○

1 Cut the turnip into round slices 1cm thick, and then cut the slices into the shape of a shuttlecock board.

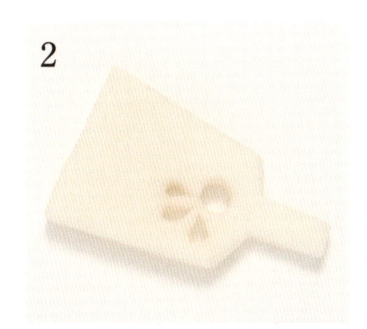

2 Carve a circle and three waterdrop shapes near the handle in the design of a shuttlecock. Cut straight through the turnip, rotating the knife and the turnip simultaneously in opposite directions. Remove the excess material.

3 Fill the circle and waterdrop shapes made in step 2 with carrots. To ensure that the size is appropriate, make the carrot's circle and waterdrop shapes slightly larger and adjust the sizes when filling.

Japanese New Year

Basket (with handle)

Small baskets with handles making full use of the cucumber's shape. A design that is perfect for the New Years.

Difficulty | ● ○ ○ ○ ○

1 Cut out a 6cm-long section from the front end of the cucumber, with its pedicle kept.

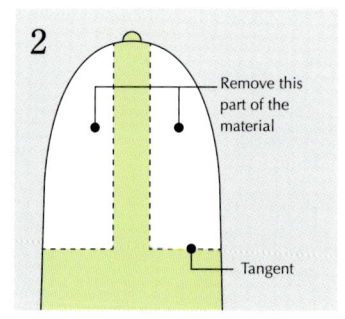

2 Use the knife to draw the outline lightly, and make the handle of the basket.

Remove this part of the material

Tangent

3 Along the outline, make a vertical cut and a horizontal cut, and remove the excess material to make a shape as shown in the picture.

4 Repeat the same process on the other side (at the back).

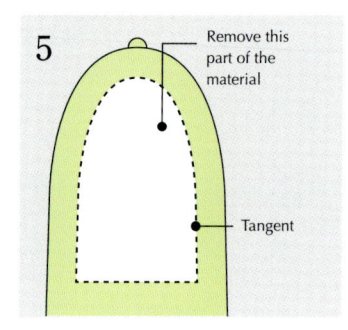

5 Draw an outline of the handle lightly with the knife.

Remove this part of the material

Tangent

6 Cut along the outline, and run the knife through.

7

Turn the knife around and remove the excess material. The handle of the basket is now completed.

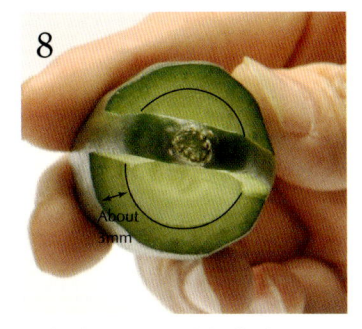

8

Make the interior of the basket. On the cross section of the cucumber, insert the knife vertically at a distance of about 3mm from the edge, and carve a circle about 5mm deep.

9

Dig a "レ"-shaped groove along the circle. The center of the basket should be trimmed neatly.

10

Carve zigzag patterns at the edge of the basket. Cut from the upper left to the lower right, and then one side of the sawtooth is completed.

11

Follow step 10 and continue to move the knife from the upper right to the lower left, carving out the other side of the sawtooth. Note that the angle, width, and size of the left and right cuts must be the same so that the finished zigzag patterns are neat and beautiful.

12

Repeat steps 10 and 11 to make a serrated lace on the entire circle.

13

Place the basket so that it is upright, and make a conical shape at the center on its outside wall.

14

Carve five conical shapes to form a plum blossom.

15

Carve a smaller plum blossom of five petals on each side of this big one. A beautiful little basket is finished.

Japanese New Year

Basket (without handle)

Present New Year's cuisine, such as black beans, in this festive basket made from cucumber.

Difficulty ● ○ ○ ○ ○

1 Cut out a 4cm-long section from the middle of the cucumber.

2 Make the interior of the basket. On the cross section of the cucumber, insert the knife vertically at a distance of about 3mm from the edge, and carve a circle about 5mm deep.

3 Dig a "レ"-shaped groove along the circle, and trim the center of the basket neatly.

4 Carve zigzag patterns at the edge of the basket. Cut from the upper left to the lower right. One side of the sawtooth is completed.

5 Follow step 4 and continue to move the knife from the upper right to the lower left, carving out the other side of the sawtooth. Note that the angle, width, and size of the left and right cuts must be the same so that the finished zigzag patterns are neat and beautiful.

6 Repeat steps 4 and 5 to make a serrated lace on the entire circle.

7 Place the basket straight, and make a conical shape at the center on its outside wall.

8 Carve five conical shapes to form a plum blossom.

9 Carve a smaller plum blossom of five petals on each side of this big one. A beautiful little basket is finished.

53

Japanese New Year

Turnip fan 1

The secret to making a beautiful fan is making sure that the fan's outer edge is cut deep and broad.

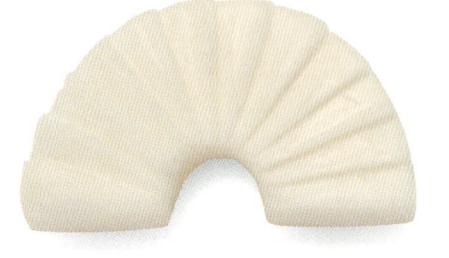

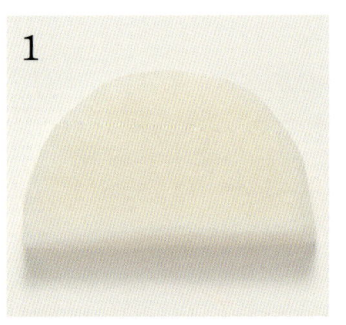

Difficulty ● ○ ○ ○ ○

1 Cut the turnip into a circle that is 1cm thick, and then cut it into semicircles.

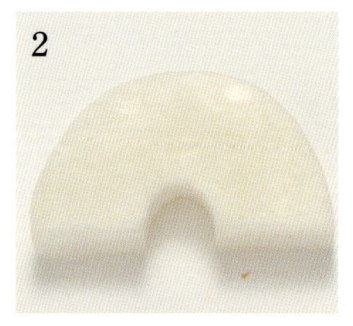

2 Cut a smaller semicircle at the center of the bigger one, and remove the excess material.

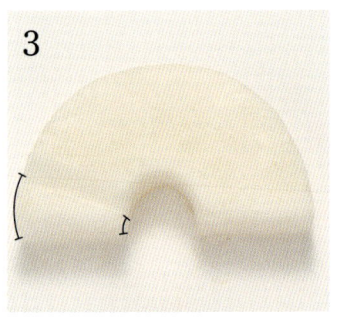

3 Cut straight lines 5mm deep in a radial arrangement on the fan. On the right-hand side of each straight line, cut out a "レ"-shaped groove. The grooves should be deeper at the outer edge of the fan.

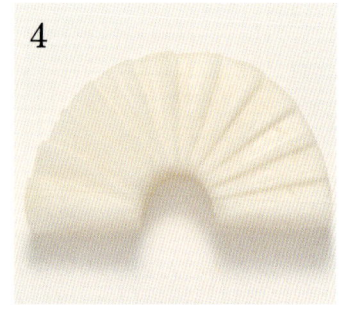

4 Repeat step 3 until the entire fan is finished.

Japanese New Year

Turnip fan 2

Use the angle to create a three-dimensional sense to highlight the impression of the fan.

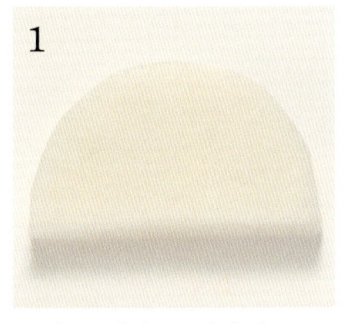

Difficulty ● ○ ○ ○ ○

1 Cut the turnip into a circle that is 1cm thick, and then cut it into semicircles.

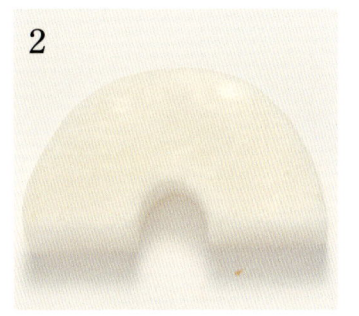

2 Carve a smaller semicircle at the center of the bigger one, and remove the excess material.

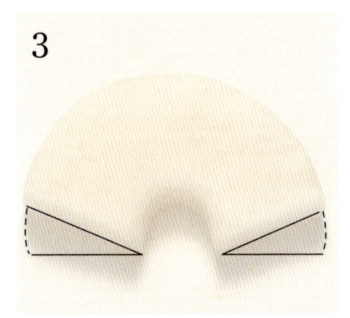

3 Cut off both ends of the fan so that there is a sense of an angle.

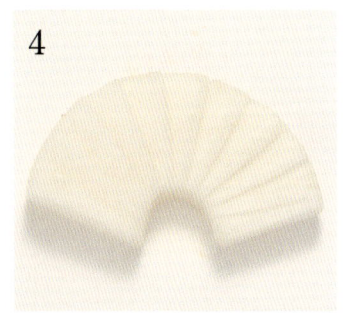

4 Cut straight lines 5mm deep in a radial arrangement on the fan. On the right-hand side of each straight line, cut out a "レ"-shaped groove. The grooves should be deeper at the outer edge of the fan. Repeat this step until the entire fan is finished.

55

Japanese New Year

Turnip crane

Place a crane in the New Year's dishes together with the turtle, as they are both symbols of longevity.

Difficulty ● ● ● ○ ○

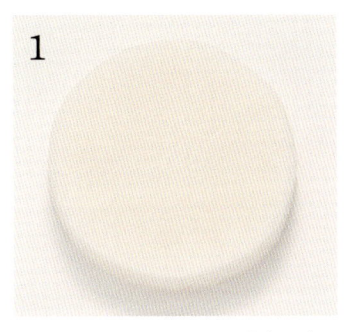

1 Cut the turnip into a round disc that is 1cm thick, and peel.

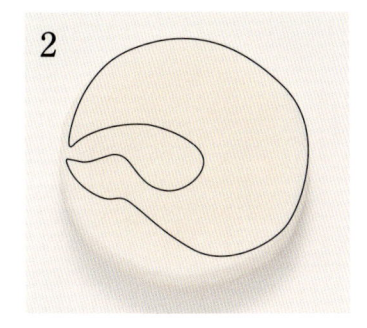

2 Use the carving knife to draw the outline of the crane gently as shown in the picture.

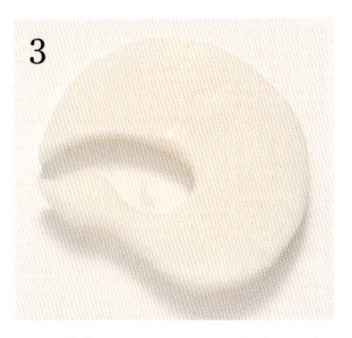

3 Cut off the excess material along the outline. Trim the rough corners of the crane's head and neck to make them smooth and polished.

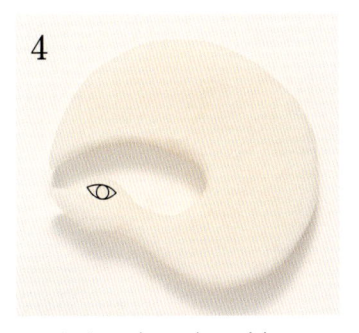

4 Gently draw the outline of the crane's eye, 3mm deep, with the carving knife, as shown in the picture. Remove the excess material inside the eye to make the eyeball more three-dimensional.

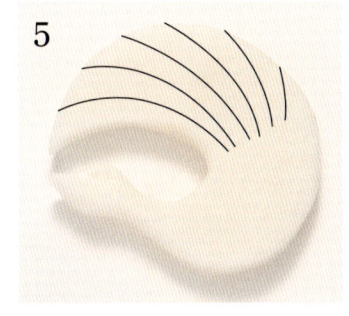

5 Gently trace the outline of the crane's feathers with the carving knife as shown in the picture.

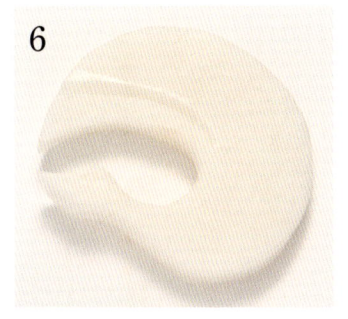

6 Cut a line 5mm deep along the outline of the feathers. Then, dig a "レ"-shaped groove on the right-hand side of the line, and remove the excess material.

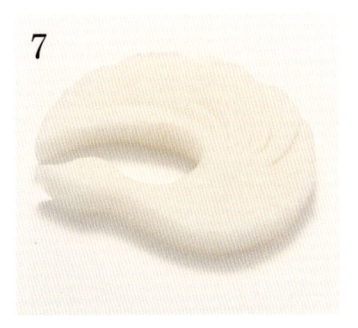

7 Repeat step 6 until the feather shape has been completed.

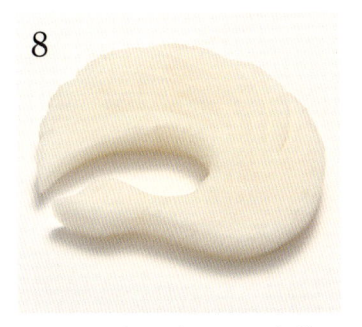

8 To create a three-dimensional effect of every feather standing up, trim the sides slightly to give the crane a sharp outline. Trim the uneven edges to make them smooth and polished.

Japanese New Year

Turnip turtle

Turtles should be displayed together with the cranes. Take care to engrave the shell with sharp, neat lines.

Difficulty	● ● ● ○ ○

1

Cut the turnip into a round disc that is 1cm thick, and peel.

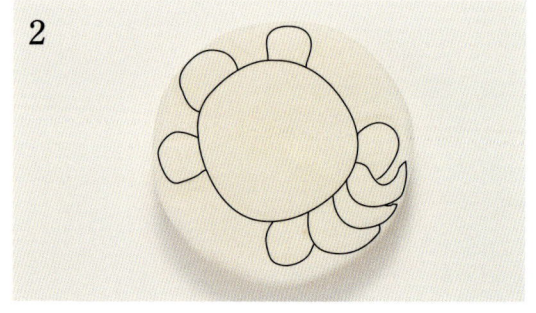

2

Use the carving knife to draw the outline of the turtle gently as shown in the picture.

3

Cut off the excess material along the outline.

4

Trace the circular outline of the turtle shell so that the shell stands out. Deepen the effect of the outline by carving a "レ"-shaped groove beside it.

5 Trim the edges of the head, shell, feet, and tail of the turtle to make them smooth and polished.

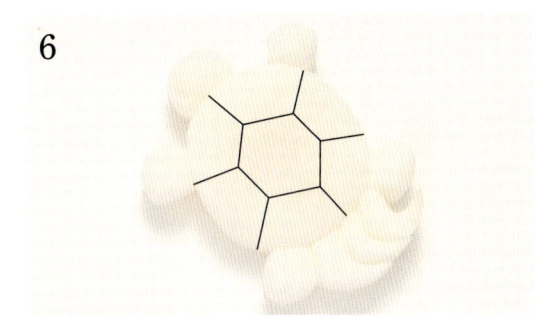

6 Gently trace the texture of the turtle shell with the carving knife as shown in the picture.

7 Deepen the hexagon at the center of the turtle shell pattern by carving a "V"-shaped groove beside its outline. The six straight lines that radiate from the vertices of the hexagon should all be carved 5mm deep.

8 Carve a smaller hexagon inside the bigger one, and deepen the outline by carving a "レ"-shaped groove beside it. The six straight lines that radiate from the vertices of the hexagon should all be carved 5mm deep.

9 In the six areas outside the hexagon, draw straight lines along the outside of the existing line, and carve a "レ"-shaped groove beside it to strengthen the effect.

10 Continue with the same process as in step 9 in the remaining five areas. The texture of the turtle shell has now been completed.

Japanese New Year

Yuzu jar (with lid)

This intricately designed, stylized lid hides wondrous secrets within.

| Difficulty | ● ● ○ ○ ○ |

60

1 Turn the carving knife around at the top ⅓ of the yuzu, taking care not to damage the pulp inside.

2 Separate the peel from the pulp with your fingers. Do not throw away this part of the peel. Instead, use it to make a lid.

3 Make the jar body in the same way as in step 2. Take off the peel, and remove the pulp.

4 Carve patterns on the yuzu. As shown in the picture, divide the edge of the skin, which will be used for making the jar body, into six equal parts, and make marks.

5 This is how it looks from the side.

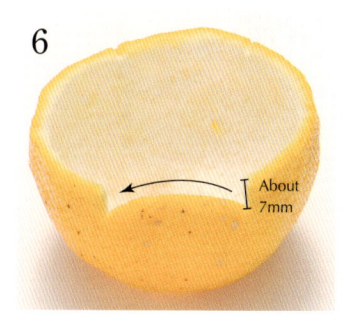

6 Cut downward from the marks to a depth of about 7mm, and carve a rounded arc between the adjacent marks.

About 7mm

7 Repeat step 6 to complete the remaining five arcs.

8 Hollow out a vertical waterdrop shape at the center of the arc, and then, hollow out two sloping waterdrops symmetrically on both sides of the vertical one. Together, they form a bamboo-leaf.

9 Repeat step 8 for the remaining five arcs. A beautiful yuzu jar is completed.

61

10 Carve patterns on the lid. The process is the same as that for the jar body. Divide the edge of the peel into six equal parts, and make marks. Cut downward from the mark to a depth of about 7mm, and carve a rounded arc between the adjacent marks.

11 Hollow out a vertical waterdrop shape at the center of the arc.

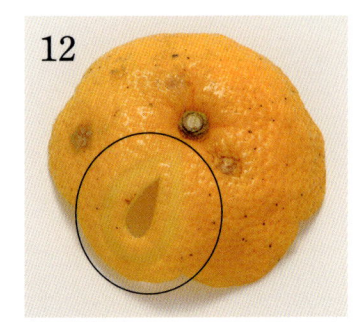

12 Carve another waterdrop shape outside the hollowed-out waterdrop, but do not hollow out this one. Then, cut out a "レ"-shaped groove along the outline of this waterdrop located at the edge.

13 Repeat step 12 for the remaining five arcs.

14 Fit the lid on the jar, and a beautiful yuzu jar is completed.

63

Japanese New Year

Yuzu jar (without lid)

Offer New Year's dishes in this yuzu jar to add freshness to the season's decorations.

Difficulty ● ● ○ ○ ○

1. Turn the carving knife around at the top ⅓ of the yuzu, taking care not to damage the pulp inside.

2. Separate the peel from the pulp with your fingers. Do not throw away this part of the peel. Instead, use it to make a lid.

3. Make the jar body in the same way as shown in step 2. Take off the peel, and remove the pulp.

4. Carve patterns on the yuzu. As shown in the picture, divide the edge of the skin, which will be used for making the jar body, into six equal parts, and make marks.

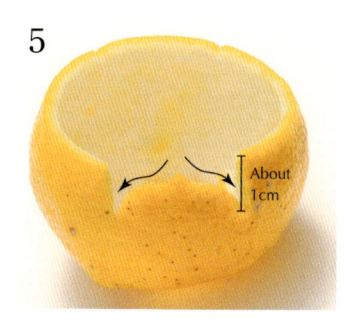

5. Cut downward from the mark to a depth of about 1cm as shown in the picture. Insert the knife between the adjacent cuts, and cut an "S"-shaped arc to each of the left- and right-hand sides.

6. Repeat step 5 for the remaining five arcs.

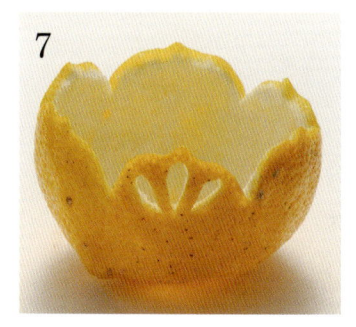

7. Hollow out a vertical waterdrop shape at the center of the arc, and then hollow out two sloping waterdrops symmetrically on both sides of the vertical one. Together they form a bamboo-leaf.

8. Repeat step 7 for the remaining five arcs. A beautiful yuzu jar is completed.

practical tips

Thai knife maintenance

Because of their thin blades and their flexibility, even specialists often refuse the job of sharpening Thai knives. When the knife is used for fruit carving, the blade rusts quickly and blacken, leaving black marks on the fruits or vegetables. Rusted blades are also difficult to work with, so regular maintenance is must.

The methods of knife maintenance:

What to prepare

Waterproof sandpaper
Three kinds of grit sizes: 500-grit, 1000-grit, 2000-grit.
※A higher number indicates finer sandpaper particles.
The sandpaper should be placed on a flat platform, and its surface should be sprinkled with a little water.

Floral foam block
Trim to the size of 2cm × 5cm × 1cm.
Putting a water-soaked floral foam block on the blade to ensure that the weight is equally distributed when pressure is applied to the knife.

Maintenance method

If the blade is rusty
Place a sheet of sandpaper on a high table and sprinkle some water on the surface. Press the blade of the knife against the sandpaper, then place a water-soaked floral foam block on top of the blade. Move the foam block and the blade simultaneously, drawing circles on the sandpaper. Use the 1000-grit first, and when the rust is gone, polish with a 2000-grit.

If the tip is broken
Polish the back of the knife at angle with a 500-grit sandpaper until the broken tip is sharp again. After sharpening the tip, polish the surface of the blade with a 2000-grit sandpaper in a circular movement.

If the blade is chipped
Use a 500-grit sandpaper to level the rest of the blade with the chipped area. Note that the blade should not be held too straight when being sharpened, or the blade will become blunt. Finish off with a 2000-grit sandpaper.

※ If the knife will not be used for a while after being sharpened, the blade should be coated with camelia oil to prevent rust. Any oil that is not easily oxidized can be used.

Hinamatsuri (Girl's Day in Japan)

Add a breath of warm spring air to celebrate the special day for girls.

67

Hinamatsuri
Spring party
In spring, everything comes to life. Make full use of brightly colored vegetables and fruits and display them on glass tableware, complete with pink tablecloths to make the scene sweet and girly.

Vegetables and fruits to be used

Melons, strawberries, oranges, colored peppers, cucumbers and carrots

Key tips

Melon bowl
The engraved melon bowl is already luxurious and eye-catching in itself, but perfect the impact by decorating its surroundings with pink peach blossoms, right in season during Hinamatsuri. Add tricolored ribbons in the colors of the diamond rice cakes made especially for this event. The light pinks and greens and perfect for spring.

Pepper tulips
Insert tulips carved from colored peppers into a glass, and combine them with engraved cucumber leaves. The vivid colors used are emblematic of plants bursting to life in spring. A butterfly carved from carrots fluttering among the flowers adds movement to the scene.

Strawberry tulips
Fill a small cocktail glass with sand the three colors of the rice cakes, and insert a tulip carved out of adorable strawberries. Because they are displayed in cocktail glasses with a little height, even if they are small the strawberries cannot be missed. Add peach blossoms to make the entire display even more sweet.

Dessert stand
A dessert stand is used for parties or afternoon tea. Because of its height, it makes the entire table display three-dimensional and dazzling. They are also ideal for charmingly displaying smaller projects. Don't forget to decorate it with peach blossoms.

Hinamatsuri

Strawberry tulips

Arrange small, cute tulips in clusters to create a beautiful image of flower fields.

| Difficulty | ● ● ○ ○ ○ |

1

Remove the leaves of the strawberries. If you like, it is also fine and lovely to keep the leaves on.

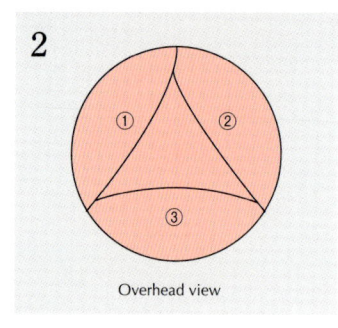

2

Overhead view

As shown in the picture, try to create the effect of three petals overlapping each other.

3

To cut the curve of the first petal on the side of the strawberry, refer to the line and cutting angle shown in the picture.

70

4

Along the line in step 3, cut a "レ"-shaped groove on the inside.

5

Carve the second petal in the same way, overlapping the first petal. Cut a "レ"-shaped groove inside the second scribed line.

6

This is how it looks after step 5.

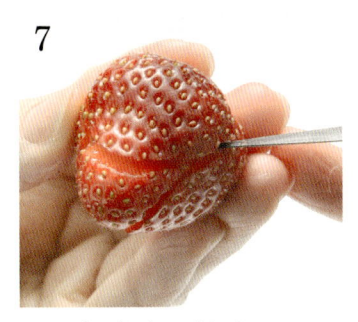

7

Carve the third petal in the same way, overlapping the second petal. Cut a "レ"-shaped groove inside the third scribed line. The three petals are completed.

8

Cut off the top of the strawberry.

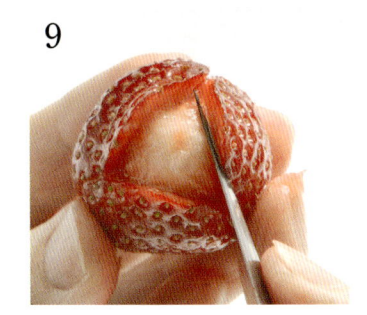

9

Shave the white pulp exposed at the top, and trim it into a round hill shape.

10

Carve a "V"-shaped groove from the middle of a petal toward the top of the white pulp.

11

Repeat step 10 to complete the remaining two sections. The three "V"-shaped grooves converge at the top, showing three small petals in the middle of the large petals.

12

This is how it looks from the side.

Hinamatsuri

Colored pepper tulips

Use the particular features of colored peppers to carve colorful tulips!

Difficulty ● ○ ○ ○ ○

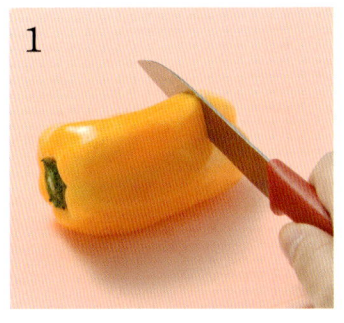

1 Cut off a ¼ of the pepper. The portion that is cut off can be used to make a pepper dish (see p. 156).

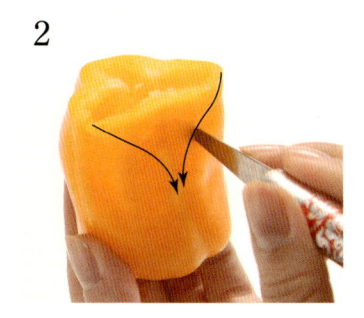

2 Along the shape of the bell pepper, cut a "V" shape.

3 Here is how it looks after cutting. Depending on the shape of the colored pepper, make three or four petals.

4 When the petals are finished, divide them from the inner part of the pepper by cutting vertically. Trim the pepper seeds, cut off the seeds that stretch around, and leave only a rounded shape at the center.

5 The center has been trimmed.

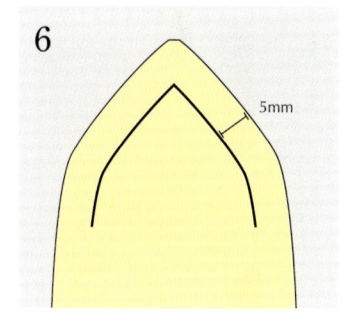

6 As shown in the picture, cut 5mm inward from the edge of the petal, note to cut through.

7 Gently pull out the 5mm-wide part cut out in step 6 to create the effect of the petal blooming outward.

8 Repeat steps 6 and 7 to complete the remaining two petals.

Hinamatsuri

Carrot butterfly

With just a little trick, make beautiful butterflies that bring spring to the table.

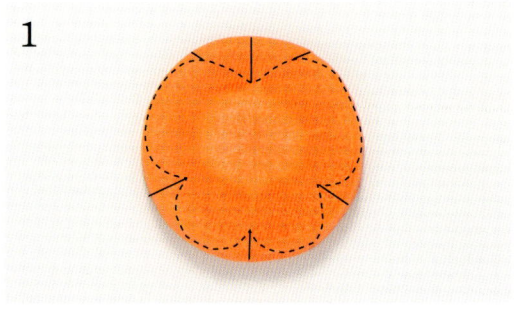

Difficulty ● ○ ○ ○ ○

1 Cut the carrot into a 5mm-thick round slice, and peel. Gently trace the outline on the slice.

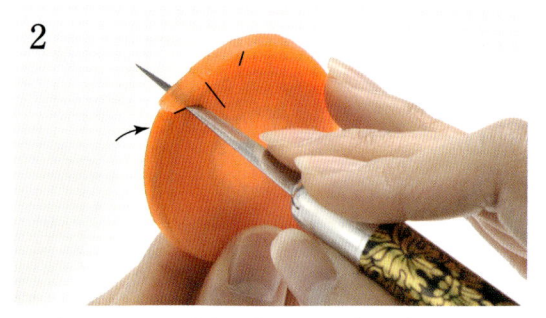

2 Cut from the upper left to the center along the contour line to carve a smooth outline.

3 Similarly, carve a smooth outline from the upper right to the center.

4 The outline of the butterfly's head is completed.

5

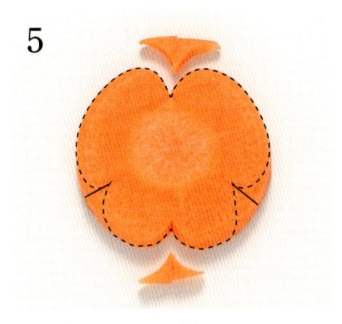

In the lower part of the carrot, follow steps 2 and 3 to continue the outline of the butterfly.

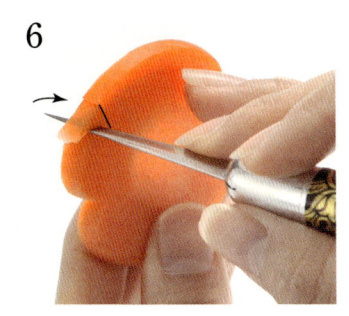

6

Carve the four wings. Along the upper left mark line, move the knife from the left-hand side to carve a smooth outline.

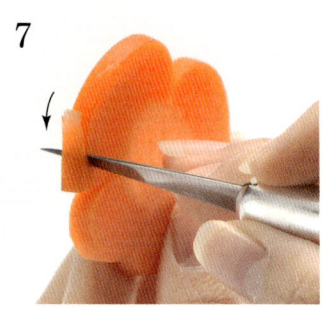

7

Similarly, move the knife from the right-hand side along the upper left mark line, and cut out the other half of the smooth outline.

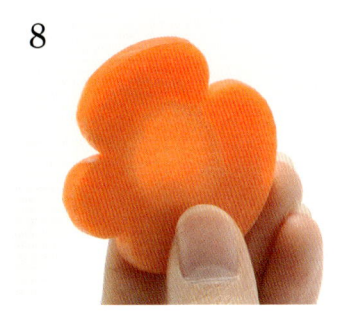

8

The middle part of the butterfly wing is completed.

9

The right-hand side is also carved in the same way as shown in steps 6 and 7. The four wings are all completed.

10

Then, make the butterfly antennae. Move the knife from the upper left to the lower right, and cut out a thin slice. Do not break it.

11

Make another cut below the line cut out in step 10.

12

Remove the excess material between the two lines in steps 10 and 11. One antenna is finished.

13

Repeat the same process on the right-hand side to finish the second antenna.

75

Hinamatsuri

Cucumber leaf 1, 2 and 3

Only the basic techniques are necessary to complete these three types of leaf decorations that freshly burnish any table.

Difficulty | ● ○ ○ ○ ○

1
Cut the cucumber into a length of 6cm.

2
Trisect the periphery of the cucumber, and cut three equal pieces. The remaining part in the middle is a triangular prism shape.

3
Trim the three slices in step 2 into the shape of leaves. Now, let's make three different leaf shapes.

4
Leaf 1: Carve the veins of the first leaf. Cut a straight line in the middle of the leaf, and carve a "V"-shaped groove.

76

5

Starting from the central part of the vein, carve an eye-like shape slantwise.

6

Repeat step 5 to create a series of eye-like shapes on both sides of the vein.

7

Starting from the side of the leaf, carve the smooth outline of the leaf along the edge of the eye-like shapes.

8

The second cut should be slightly tilted. Move the knife from the upper right-hand side to the lower left-hand side.

9

Remove the excess material. Repeat steps 7 and 8 to complete the carving on the right-hand side.

10

Repeat the same process on the left-hand side. The first cut should be along the edge of the eye-like shapes, to carve the smooth outline of the leaf.

11

The second cut should be made by moving the knife from the upper left-hand side to the lower right-hand side, to carve the detailed lines.

12

This is how it looks after the excess material is removed.

13

Repeat steps 10 and 11 to complete the carving on the left-hand side. The first leaf is finished.

14

Leaf 2: Make the veins of the second leaf. Cut two straight lines in the middle that are 3mm deep, and which meet at the top of the leaf. Carve a "レ"-shaped groove on the outer side of each straight line.

15

Carve a "V"-shaped groove slantwise from the central vein outward.

16

Repeat step 15 to carve "V"-shaped grooves on each side. The closer the "V" shape to the top of the leaf the smaller it should be.

17

Make the contour of the leaf. Make the first cut along the outer side of the "V"-shaped groove to carve a smooth curve.

18

The second cut should be a little slanted. Move the knife from the upper right-hand side to the lower left-hand side.

19

This is how it looks after removing the excess material. Repeat steps 17 and 18 to complete the right-hand side.

20 Repeat the same process on the left-hand side. The first cut is made to carve a smooth curve along the outer side of the "V"-shaped groove.

21 The second cut should be a little slanted. Move the knife from the upper right-hand side to the lower left-hand side.

22 This is how it looks after removing the excess material.

23 Repeat steps 20 and 21 to complete the left-hand side. The second leaf is completed.

24 Leaf 3: Make the veins of the third leaf. Carve a "V"-shaped groove as the central vein.

25 Carve "V"-shaped grooves alternately on both sides of the central vein.

26 Repeat step 25 to complete the leaf veins on both sides. The closer the "V" shape is to the top of the leaf the smaller it is.

27 Make the contour of the leaf. Make the first cut along the outer side of the "V"-shaped groove to carve a smooth curve.

28 The second cut should be a little slanted. Move the knife from the upper right-hand side to the lower left-hand side.

29 This is how it looks after removing the excess material. Repeat steps 27 and 28 to complete the right-hand side.

30 Perform the same process on the left-hand side. The first cut is made to carve a smooth curve along the outer side of the "V"-shaped groove.

31 The second cut should be made by moving the knife from the upper left-hand side to the lower right-hand side, to carve the detailed lines.

32 Here is how it looks after removing the excess material. Repeat steps 30 and 31 to complete the left-hand side.

33 The third leaf is completed.

34 The leaf shapes 1, 2 and 3 have all been completed.

Make pickles from carved carrots or red peppers.

Homemade pickles are easily made with pickling brine water from the market. Pack the carved vegetables in bottles or jars, preferably of the same height. Add the pickling brine water, making sure all the vegetables are fully submerged. The vegetables will float, so the key is to make sure the jars are packed, leaving no space. Soak for an hour for a mild taste. For a stronger taste, keep the vegetable soaked for 12 to 24 hours.

81

Hinamatsuri

Orange basket

An orange basket with a very stylish handle.
Two baskets can be made out of one orange.

Difficulty | ● ○ ○ ○ ○

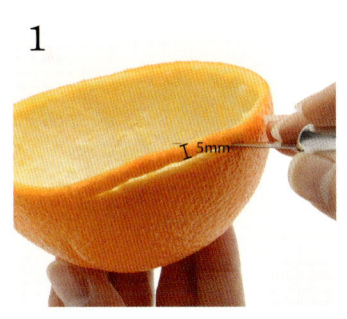

1 Split the orange crossways into two halves, peel them, and remove the pulp (see p. 61). Carve a line parallel to the edge of the orange peel that is 5mm below the edge.

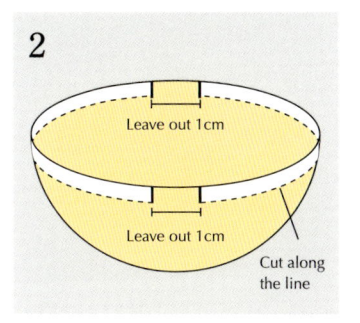

2 As shown in the picture, step 1 does not involve engraving a complete circle as 1cm is left in each of the two positions facing each other.

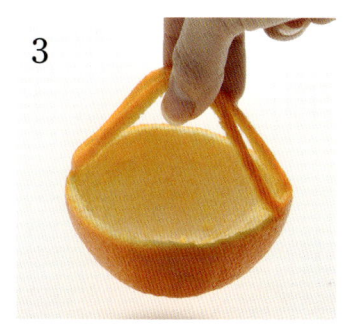

3 The handle of the basket is completed.

4 Carve zigzag lines on the edge of the basket. First carve a line from the upper left-hand side to the lower right-hand side.

5 Carve another line from the upper right-hand side to the lower left-hand side in front of the line carved out in step 4.

6 One serrated lace is finished. For aesthetic reasons, the angles, widths, and sizes of the left and right lines should be as consistent as possible.

7 Repeat steps 4 and 5 to complete the entire serrated lace. Attach a ribbon bow to the handle, place the pulp that was removed in step 1 into the basket, and decorate it with mint leaves. The work is completed.

Hinamatsuri

Melon bowl

Use an entire melon to create a gorgeous art piece sure to be the highlight of any party display.

Difficulty ● ● ● ● ○

1

Prepare a melon.

2

Divide the melon horizontally into two. One half is used to carve a bowl, and the pulp of the other half is later served in it.

3

Scoop out all the melon seeds with a spoon.

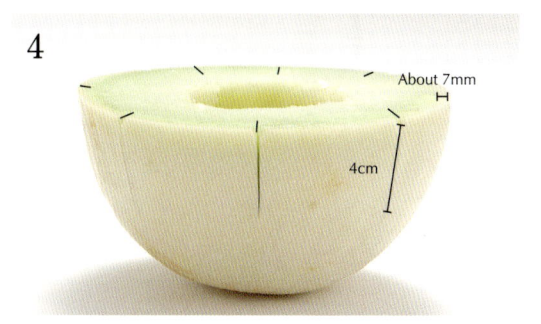

4

Draw eight equally marked lines on the edge of the melon. Cut about 7mm inward from the edge. The depth of the incision is 4cm.

5

Cut a 4cm-deep circle about 7mm from the edge. Link the eight lines cut out in step 4.

6

Cut from the middle of the two adjacent eight-divided tangents. An "S" curve is carved on each side to form a petal outside the bowl wall.

7

Repeat step 6 to complete the eight petals.

8

Divide the cross section of the melon into eight equal parts. Cut downward from the vertex of the petal located on the outside to a depth of 1–2cm.

9

Trim the eight equal parts of the pulp to make the outline of the bowl polished.

10

The dome shape, as shown in the picture, is completed.

11

Repeat step 9 to finish the remaining seven parts. The eight dome shapes are all completed.

12

Carve a rose on every other dome. On the side of the dome shape, carve the first petal. Make another cut slantwise inside it, and remove the excess material between the two cuts. Next, carve the second petal to slightly overlap the first one. Make another cut slantwise inside it, and remove the excess material between the two cuts.

13

Two petals have been finished.

14

Repeat step 12 to complete the remaining three petals.

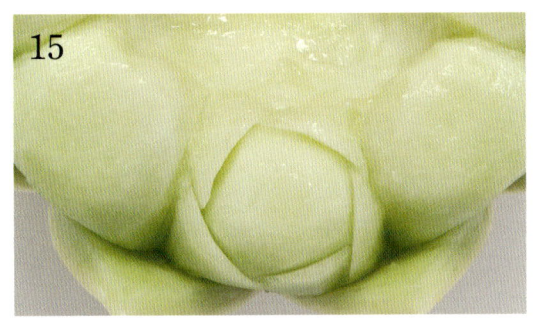

15

Trim the areas enclosed by the petals to make it smooth and polished.

16

Carve the second layer of petals. Repeat step 12 to complete the remaining four petals.

17

Repeat step 15 to trim the shape of the dome. Then, make a third layer of petals. Repeat step 12 to complete three petals. The rose is completed.

18

Repeat steps 12 through 17 on every other dome to complete the remaining three roses.

19

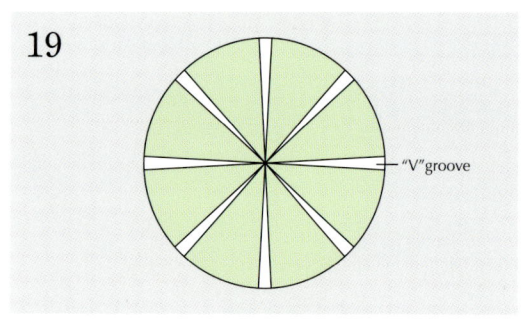

"V" groove

On the remaining four dome shapes, draw the shape of whipped cream being squeezed out. Then cut eight "V"-shaped grooves from the outside to the inside as shown in the picture.

20

Carve the third line as shown in the picture.

21

This is how it looks after eight lines have been carved.

22

Repeat step 19. Draw the shape of whipped cream being extruded on the remaining three dome shapes.

23

Scoop out a few pulp balls with the melon baller from the other half of the melon as mentioned in step 2.

24

Place the pulp balls made in step 23 in the melon bowl, and add some mint leaves for decoration. The whole work is now completed.

Halloween

Light up the jack-o'-lanterns when nighttime comes to create the perfect atmosphere for Halloween.

Halloween

Pumpkin toy box

Display the orange pumpkins against an eerie black background to make them really stand out. Add some uncarved pumpkins to double the fun!

Vegetables and fruits to be used

Halloween pumpkins, squashes, butternut squashes, decorative pumpkins and cherry radishes

Key tips

Bat-carved pumpkins
A pumpkin engraved with a Halloween bat. This is more than enough as decoration, but add a candle or light inside the pumpkin and face the bat engraving towards the wall, and the bat-shaped light will be reflected there. There is more than one way to enjoy this piece.

Trick or treat
"Trick or Treat!" engraved boldly on the surface of a pumpkin. Exquisite, detailed designs or impulsive, daring designs—they both enlighten the Halloween spirit. Feel free to try out different words and motifs here.

Pumpkin face
There is no Halloween without the jack-o'-lantern. Jack-o'-lanterns with asymmetrical eyes, large mouths, and comical expressions. Make a variety of jack-o'-lanterns with different faces for a unique Halloween display.

Jack-o'-lantern carved with cherry radishes
Carve two eyes and a mouth on a cherry radish. Although very small, it can also be an authentic jack-o'-lantern. In a festive orange and black world of assorted pumpkins, the radish will stand out with its striking red.

Halloween

Carrot jack-o'-lantern

Jack-o'-lanterns are usually made from pumpkins, but why not try making them from carrots?

| Difficulty | ● ● ○ ○ ○ |

1 Cut the carrot into a disc that is 3cm thick and peel it.

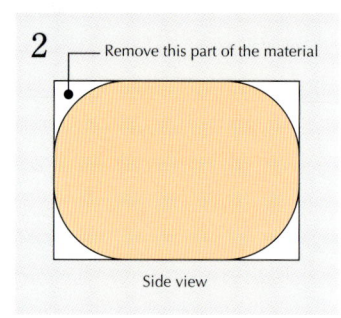

2 As shown in the picture, trim the upper and lower edges and corners to make them smooth and polished.

Remove this part of the material

Side view

3 Insert the knife vertically and cut 5mm deep on the side of the carrot.

92

4

Carve a "レ"-shaped groove on each side of the line cut in step 3.

5

Trim the cut to make it smooth and polished.

6

Repeat steps 3 through 5. Although there are eight lines in the picture, it is possible to cut as many lines as you like in the actual process. The spacing does not have to be regular.

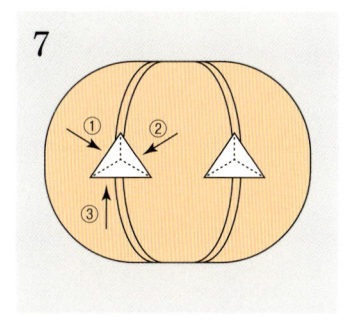

7

Next, carve the eyes. As shown in the picture, carve two eyes on the side of the pumpkin. Pay attention to the cutting angle. The edge of the knife should be tilted so that the shape you cut out is a pyramid.

8

The first cut.

9

The second cut.

10

The third cut.

11

The three cuts join together to form a pyramid. Remove the excess material within this area.

12

The two eyes are completed.

93

Halloween

Alternative jack-o'-lanterns

Jack-o'-lanterns made from persimmons, cherry radishes and butternut squash.

Difficulty | ● ○ ○ ○ ○

1

Persimmon: Carve two eyes on the side of the persimmon. Pay attention to the cutting angle, with the knife edge inclined so that the shape you cut out is a pyramid.

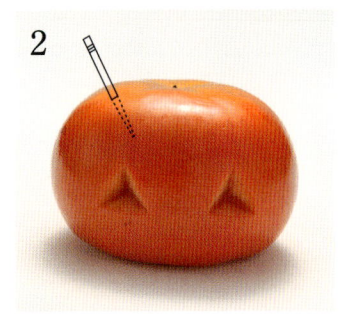

2

Insert a toothpick diagonally above the persimmon.

3

Cut off the top of a colored bell pepper. The cut line should be in a zigzag pattern. Remove the pepper seeds.

4

With the persimmon wearing the colored bell pepper on the toothpick diagonally like a hat, the work is completed.

5

Cherry radish: Follow step 1 to carve the eyes on the cherry radish. Then, following the picture, carve the outline of the teeth under the eyes. The contour outline is as shown in the picture, and each section of the line has a depth of 5mm.

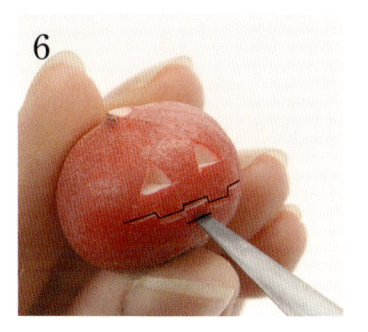

6

Carve a cross section of the outline of the lower teeth. As shown in the picture, the carving knife is parallel to the center position of the upper teeth, and the knife is tilted so that the cutting line is deep enough to intersect with the outline carved in step 5.

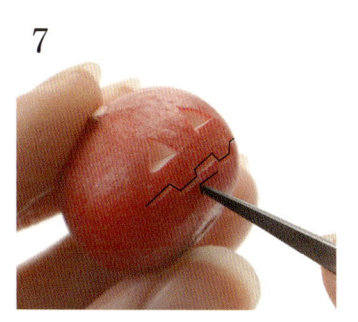

7

Insert the knife vertically to carve the vertical section of the outline of the lower teeth.

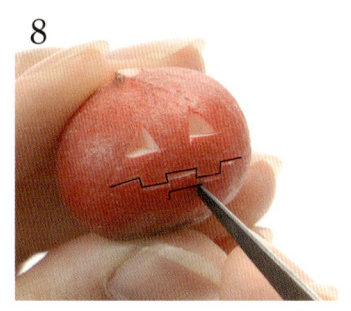

8

Carve the vertical line on the other side in the same way.

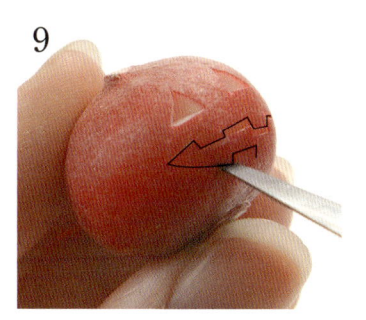

9

The vertical line on the left-hand side of the lower teeth converges with the left edge of the outline of the upper teeth. The cut here should be deep enough to intersect with the outline of the upper teeth carved in step 5.

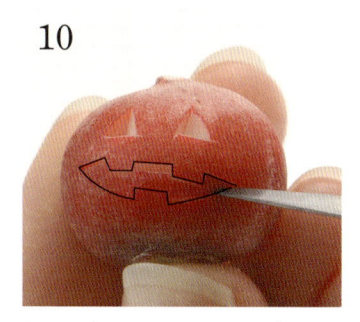

10

Repeat the same process on the right-hand side to complete the joining of the right vertical line of the lower teeth with the rightmost line of the upper teeth contour. The cut here should be deep enough to intersect with the outline of the upper teeth carved in step 5.

11

Remove the material inside of the mouth shape.

12

The cherry radish jack-o'-lantern is completed.

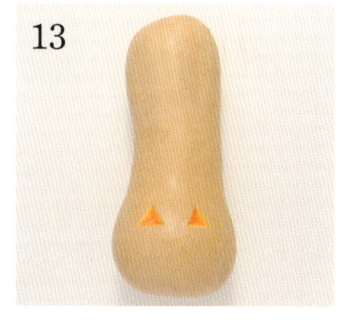

13

Butternut squash: Follow step 1 to carve eyes on the butternut squash, and the work is completed.

95

Halloween

Halloween pumpkin lantern

As long as the basic techniques are mastered, any design is possible!

| Difficulty | ●● ○ ○ ○ |

"Halloween pumpkin"—best for carving

Ordinary pumpkins can also be used, but Halloween pumpkins are softer than normal pumpkins. They also have more interior space and thinner skin, which makes carving easier. However, Halloween pumpkins spoil easily after being carved and cannot be preserved for a long time. It's best to start carving on the day before Halloween.

96

1. Holding the knife vertically, cut out a large circle at the bottom of the pumpkin.

2. Remove the pumpkin skin and pulp from this round area.

3. Use a spoon to clean out the pulp inside the pumpkin. Do not leave any residue.

4. Paste a paper stencil of the letters that you would like to make in the place where you want to carve.

5. Cut along the stencil 5mm deep. If it is a hollow letter, such as "o," "e," or "a," start from the hollow part of the letter.

6. The carving of the outline of the letters is completed.

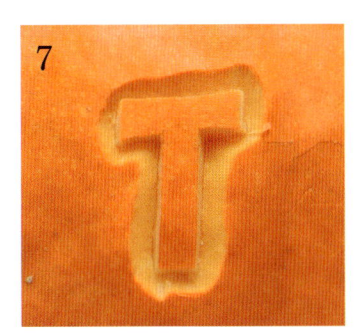

7. Carve a "レ"-shaped groove on the outside of each letter.

8. Repeat step 7 to carve all letters so that the overall effect becomes more three-dimensional. Then, carve a background around the words to match the atmosphere of the content. The work is completed.

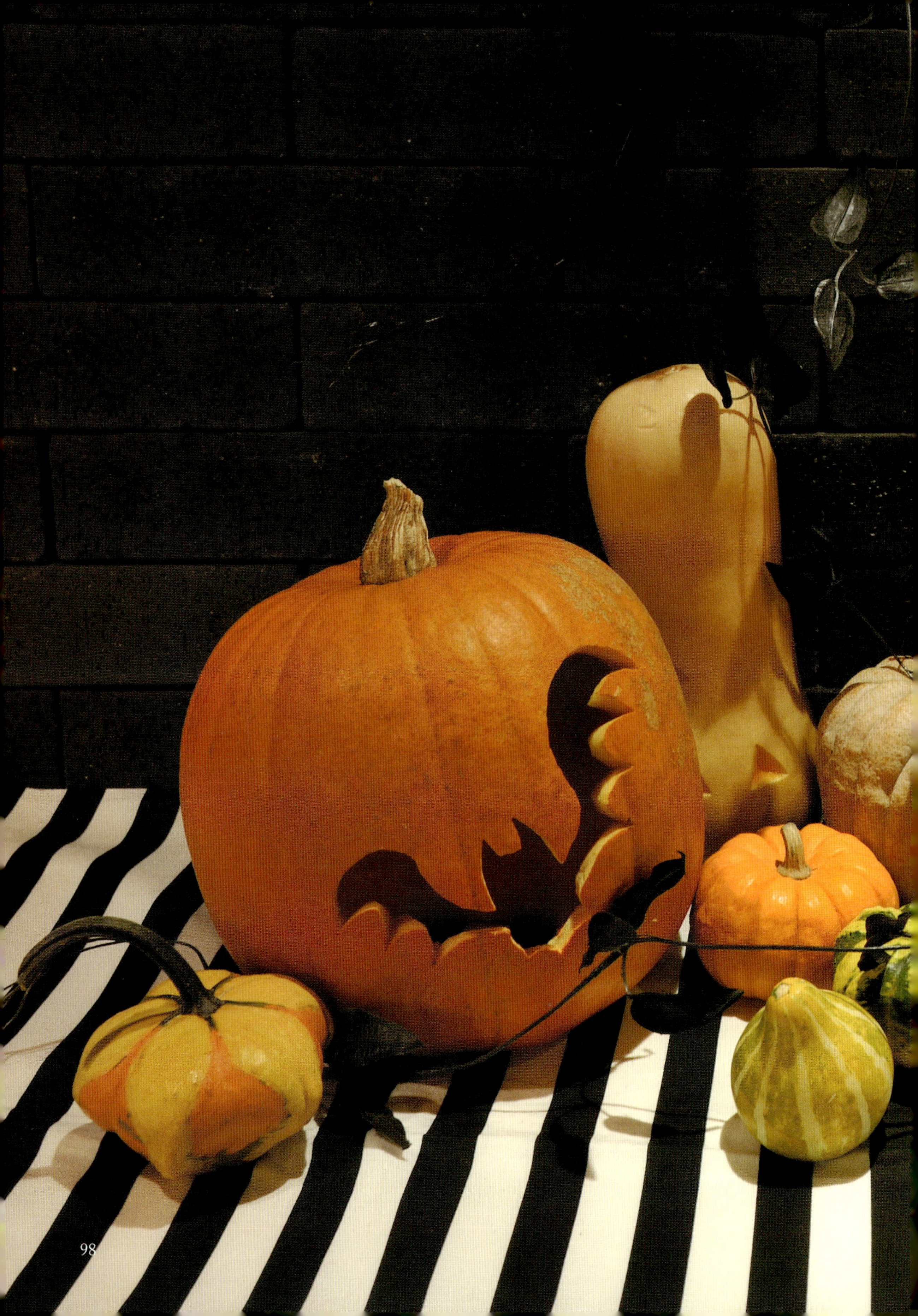

99

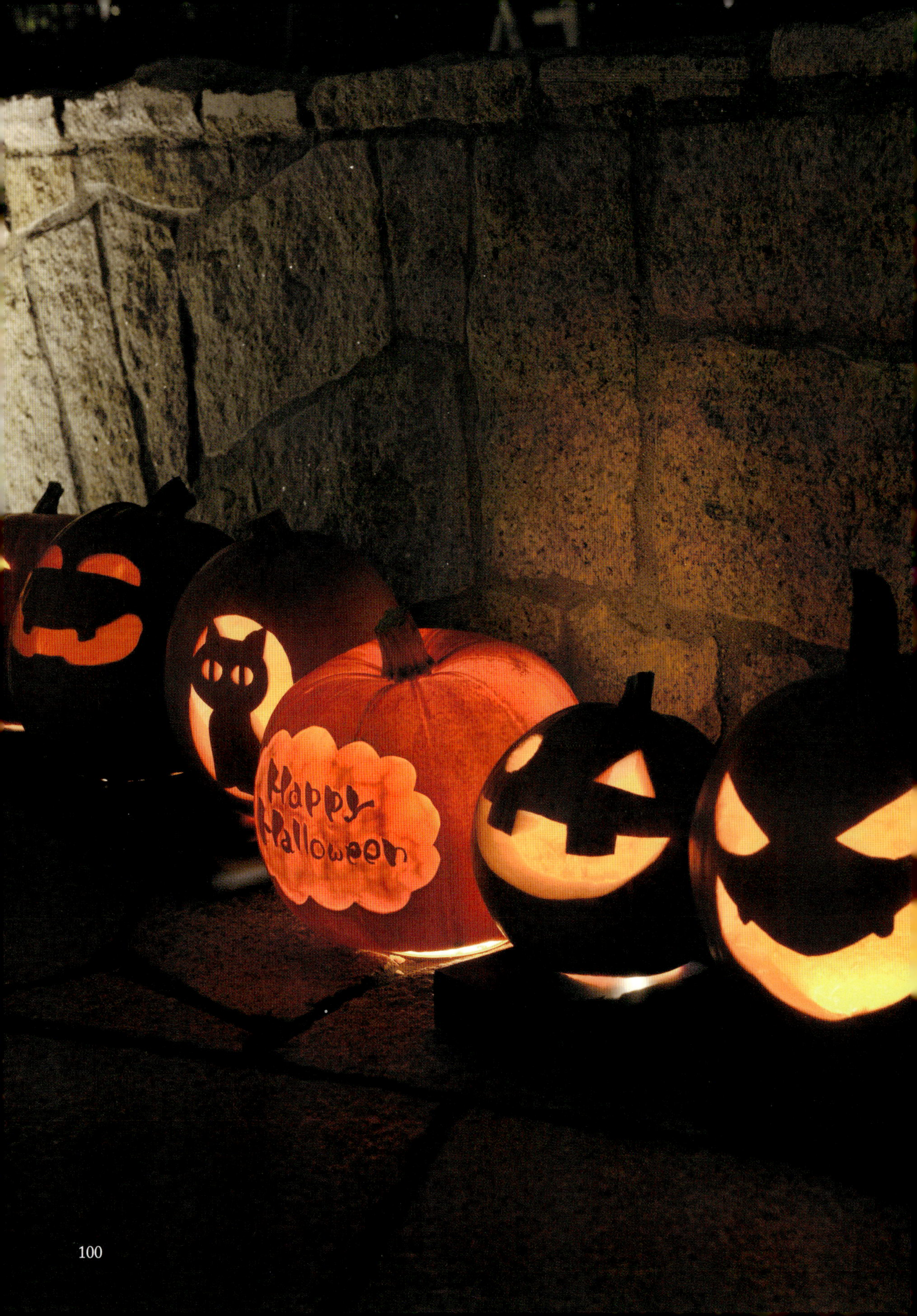
Happy
Halloween

The back of the pumpkin (the side facing the wall) can also be hollowed out with patterns or designs so that when the pumpkin is lit up, the patterns will be projected on the wall.

101

Halloween

Flower carved lantern

Put lanterns or candles inside a pumpkin to create brilliant flowers of light.

Difficulty ● ● ○ ○ ○

1 Use a carving knife to cut a circle at the top ⅓ of the orange, taking care not to injure the pulp inside.

2 Carefully separate the peel from the pulp with your fingers. The peel of the upper part is like a small lid.

3 Use a large spoon to carefully separate the peel from the pulp of the remaining ⅔ part of the orange. Be careful not to hurt the pulp. Make a gap between the pulp and peel first, and then, turn it left and right to remove the pulp. The white pith inside the peel must also be cleaned up.

4 Cut through the peel to hollow out a circle in the middle of the bottom of the peel and eight eye-like shapes around the circle.

5 Repeat step 4, and randomly carve the same shape on the side. The work is completed.

In addition to putting candles in lanterns, you can also use small lights as shown in the picture. They are available on the market.

Halloween

Heart carved lantern

Hollowed-out heart shapes are spread around the lantern, making the light warm and lovely.

Difficulty ● ● ○ ○ ○

1 Use a carving knife to cut a circle at the top ⅓ of the grapefruit, taking care not to injure the pulp inside. Carefully separate the peel from the pulp with your fingers. The peel of the upper part is like a small lid.

2 Use a large spoon to carefully separate the peel from the pulp of the remaining ⅔ part of the grapefruit. Be careful not to hurt the pulp. Make a gap between the pulp and peel first and then turn it left and right to remove the pulp. The white pith inside the peel must also be cleaned up.

3 Cut through the peel to hollow out a heart shape in the middle of the bottom of the peel.

4 Continue to randomly hollow out heart shapes.

5 When the hollowed-out heart shapes are spread all around the lantern, the work is completed.

Halloween

Cross carved lantern

Hollow out eye-like shapes in a regular pattern to create highly artistic designs.

Difficulty ● ● ○ ○ ○

1 Use a carving knife to cut a circle at the top ⅓ of the orange, taking care not to injure the pulp inside.

2 Carefully separate the peel from the pulp with your fingers. The peel of the upper part is like a small lid.

3 Use a larger spoon to carefully separate the peel from the pulp of the remaining ⅔ part of the orange. Be careful not to hurt the pulp. Make a gap between the pulp and the peel first and then turn it left and right to remove the pulp. The white pith inside the peel must also be cleaned up.

4 Cut through the peel to hollow out an eye-like shape in an orderly manner all over the peel, and the work is completed.

Halloween
Triangle carved lantern

The triangles are interwoven to create a design of geometric beauty.

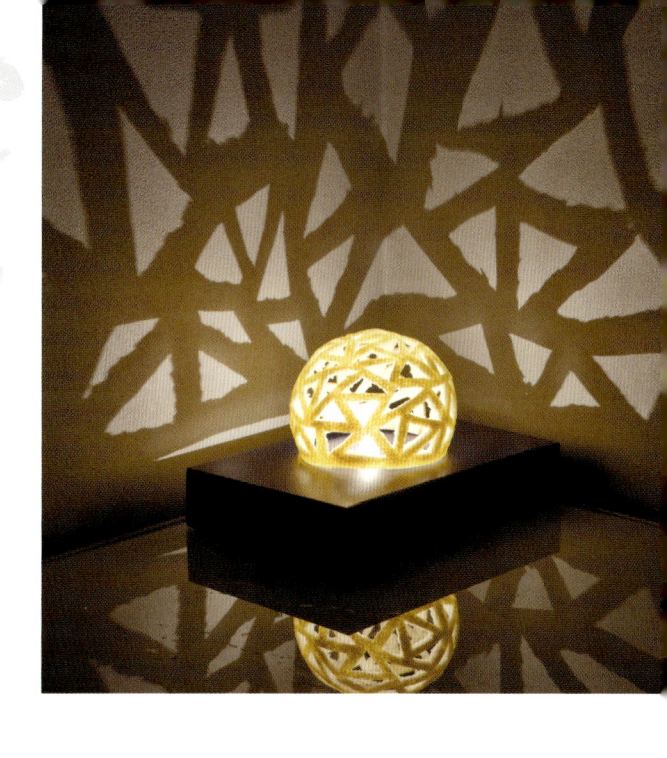

| Difficulty | ● ● ○ ○ ○ |

1 Use a carving knife to cut a circle at the top ⅓ of the grapefruit taking care not to injure the pulp inside.

2 Carefully separate the peel from the pulp with your fingers. The peel of the upper part is like a small lid.

3 Use a large spoon to carefully separate the peel from the pulp of the remaining part. Be careful not to hurt the pulp. Make a gap between the pulp and the peel first and turn it left and right to remove the pulp. The white fibers inside the peel must be cleaned up.

4 Cut through the peel to hollow out a triangle in the middle of the bottom of the peel.

5 Continue to hollow out triangles. The spacing between adjacent triangles should be as consistent as possible.

6 After the entire peel has been hollowed out, the work is completed.

Halloween

Fireworks carved lantern

The firework design should be bigger on the lower rows to create a fantastic effect with the lights.

Difficulty ● ● ○ ○ ○

1. Use a carving knife to cut a circle at the top ⅓ of the orange, taking care not to injure the pulp inside.

2. Carefully separate the peel from the pulp with your fingers. Remove the peel of the upper part, which is like a small lid.

3. Use a large spoon to carefully separate the peel from the pulp of the remaining part. Be careful not to hurt the pulp. Make a gap between the pulp and the peel first and turn it left and right to remove the pulp. The white pith inside the peel must be cleaned up.

4. Cut through the peel to hollow out a circle in the middle of the bottom of the peel and eight eye-like shapes around the circle.

5. Continue to hollow out the eight eye-like shapes of the second circle. Each shape should be slightly larger and should be located between the two shapes of the first circle.

6. Continue to hollow out the third, fourth circles of eye-like shapes. The farther the outward part the bigger the eye-like shapes until they spread all the way to the bottom of the peel.

Christmas

Artistically designed apples adds a stylish touch to Christmas.

Christmas

Apple Christmas tree

A white Christmas tree can bring out the beauty of the red apples. Apples are displayed on the stand to look like a Christmas tree.

Vegetables and fruits to be used

Apples

Key tips

Apples placed in the upper and lower rows
The Apples with carvings on the top should be place on the highest and lowest tray. This display is centered around the stem of the apple and diverges outwards. It is a very artistic display. The petals of different sizes and the hearts carved from apple peels add a little sweetness.

Apples placed in the middle row
Apples placed in the middle row should be those with carvings on the side. By placing them alternately with the apples on the top row, variety is added to the overall display. Because there is more space for carving on the side, it can highlight the delicateness of the design.

Carved apples with oriental-style shapes
Delicate lines are carved in the red peels to form a line of small triangular shapes. With the technique described here, the design is carved in one go without removing the knife from the apple. Because the peels are fragile and vulnerable, they require a lot of skill to work with, but when the completed works are displayed together, the final effect can be visually impressive.

Carved apples with firework motif
Whether from an over view or a side view, these fireworks look beautiful. Because this design only involves repeating basic techniques of eye-like sculpting, it's not difficult. The key is to make some changes to the size of eye-like shapes for every row. The size of the shapes on each row should be same.

Christmas

Forest Christmas

A Christmas display in the image of a Nordic forest. The calm wood ornaments, the sweet apples and wool balls create a peaceful and warm mood.

Vegetables and fruits to be used

Apples

Key tips

Apples
It is recommended to use apples designed with large patterns rather than ones with delicate patterns for this display. They blend in with the natural surroundings created by wood and bring out the simplicity of the overall image.

Herbal-themed white fabric
The aim is to create the image of a snow-capped winter forest. A white, flower motif cloth that will not distract from the main piece, the apple, should be used. The mood is one of gentleness and nostalgia.

Trees and pine cones
Wooden ormaments that go well with apples are effectively used in this display. Wooden plates, pine cones and Christmas tress are used to express a natural environment. Tranquil shades of brown should be used. The highlight of this winter scene is the pine cone with one corner covered in snow.

Wool balls
Although very cute, there is a sense of cold in this simple design made with apples and trees. This is why the wool is added to the scene. A small scarf or gloves, or other knitted items can also be used to add a feeling of warmth.

111

Christmas

Fireworks

Only the basic technique of eye-like carving is necessary for this piece.

Difficulty ● ● ○ ○ ○

1

Draw twelve equally divided marking lines at the top of the apple.

2

Carve an eye-like shape on one of the marking lines made in step 1.

112

3

Repeat step 2 to complete twelve eye-like shapes.

4

Continue to carve the second circle of eye-like shapes between the two adjacent shapes in the first circle. The eye-like shape should be widened to match the width of the apple.

5

Repeat step 4 to complete the second circle of eye-like shapes.

6

Make the third circle of eye-like shapes between the two adjacent shapes of the second circle. This circle is even wider than the second one.

7

Continue to carve the circles of eye-like shapes in the same way. The number of circles depends on the size of the apple. The fuller the apple the wider the shapes. When the entire carving is finished, the work is completed.

Christmas

Flowers and diamonds

A lovely pattern of eye-like designs and diamonds.

Difficulty ● ● ○ ○ ○

1

Draw six equally divided marking lines at the top of the apple.

2

Carve an eye-like shape on one of the marking lines made in step 1.

3

Repeat step 2 to complete six eye-like shapes.

4

Based on the illustrated lines, outline the outside of the eye-like shapes with a line 3mm deep.

5

Carve a "レ"-shaped groove along the outside of the outline in step 4.

6

To cut out a diamond shape, cut a cross 1cm deep between the two adjacent eye-like shapes.

7

Carve a triangle in the upper left-hand side of the cross and remove the excess material. Do the same in the upper right-hand side. Note that the two diagonal lines in the upper left-hand side and the upper right-hand side should be slightly concave to match the arc of the eye-like shapes.

8

The two diagonal lines in the lower left-hand side and the lower right-hand side should be slightly convex, like the outline of a flower petal.

9 Remove the excess material inside to form a diamond shape.

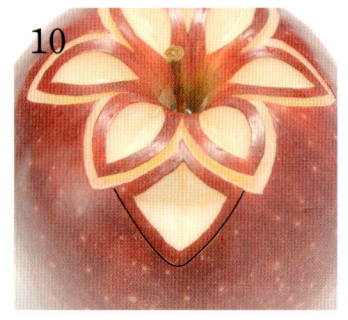

10 Trace the outline of the diamond shapes 5mm deep as shown in the picture. The key is to have the tips of the eye-like shapes stick out from the point of intersection with the diamond shape.

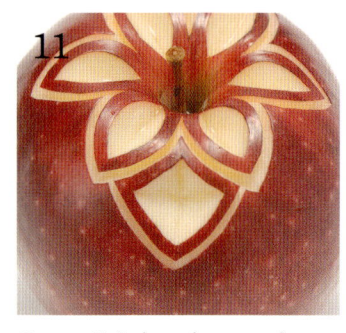

11 Carve a "レ"-shaped groove along the outside of the outline in step 10.

12 Repeat steps 6 through 11 to complete a circle of diamond shapes.

13 Frame the design by carving a line 5mm deep. using the line in the picture as an example.

14 Carve a "レ"-shaped groove along the outside of the outline in step 13.

15 Carve another line to outline the line made in step 14, using the line in the picture as an example.

16 Carve a "レ"-shaped groove along the outside of the outline in step 15, and the entire piece is finished.

Christmas

Hearts and waterdrops

A pattern of cute red hearts, adding sweetness to Christmas.

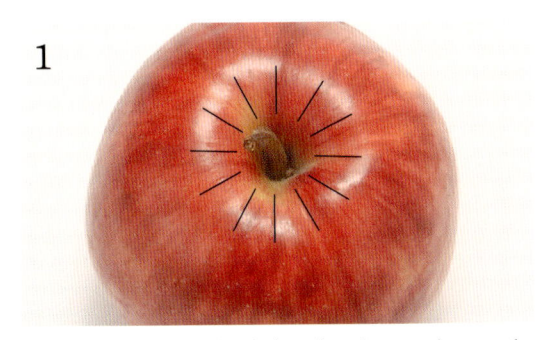

Difficulty ● ● ● ○ ○

1 Draw twelve equally divided marking lines at the top of the apple.

2 Carve an eye-like shape on one of the marking lines made in step 1.

3

Repeat step 2 to complete twelve eye-like shapes.

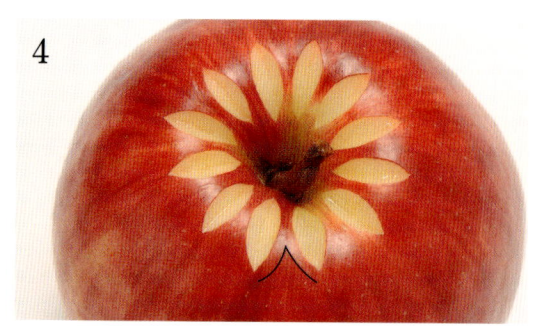

4

Using the line in the picture as an example, draw two lines, 5mm deep, on the outside of the eye-like shape.

5

Use these two lines as edges to carve a triangle 5mm deep.

6

Carve a heart below the triangle. Make a cut in the middle of the triangle, then carve a gentle slope towards its center from both the bottom left corner of the triangle and from the bottom right corner, picturing the gentle curve of a heart.

7

Following the illustrated line, carve the outline of a heart 5mm deep starting from a point slightly within the two corners of the triangle.

8

Carve a "レ"-shaped groove from the left bottom corner of the triangle towards the line carved in step 7. Note that the "V"-shaped line at the lower part of the heart should be smooth.

9

Do the same for the right side of the heart. Note that the "V"-shaped line at the lower part of the heart should be smooth.

10

Repeat steps 4 through 9 to complete a circle of hearts. Leave a little peel between the two adjacent hearts.

11

Frame the hearts with a line 5mm deep using the lines in the picture as an example.

12

Carve a "レ"-shaped groove along the outer side of the line carved in step 11.

13

Carve three waterdrops between the two adjacent hearts.

14

Repeat step 13 to complete a circle of waterdrop shapes, and the work is finished.

119

Christmas

Hearts and flowers 1

Two waterdrop shape are combined to make a heart pattern.
A step up to master the applied techniques.

Difficulty ● ● ● ● ○

1

Carve six equally divided marking lines, 5mm deep, in the middle of the side of the apple.

2

On both sides of the marked lines shown in step 1, cut slantwise and remove the peel and pulp.

120

3

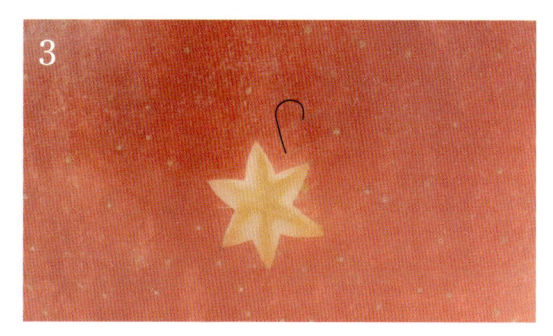

Carve a heart shape outside of the flower. Cut clockwise from the lower end of the heart, and stop at the center of the top of the heart. This is similar to carving a waterdrop shape.

4

Use the same process on the other side. Cut counterclockwise from the lower end of the heart, and stop at the center of the top of the heart. Steps 3 and 4 have no fixed sequence. Either of the two steps can be performed first.

5

Complete steps 3 and 4, and remove the excess material.

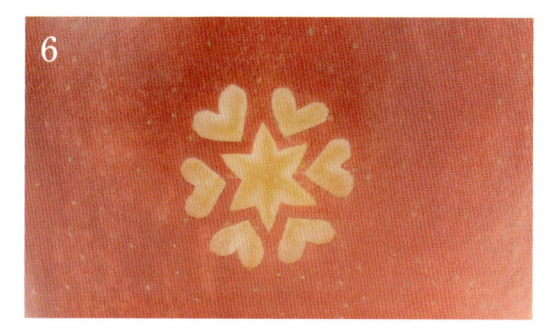

6

Repeat steps 3 and 4 to complete the remaining five shapes.

7

Carve a waterdrop shape between two adjacent hearts made in step 6.

8

Repeat step 7 to complete the remaining five shapes.

9

Carve three waterdrop shapes at the outer side of the heart made in step 6. The waterdrop in the middle should be a little bigger than the other two.

10

Repeat step 9 to complete the remaining five shapes.

11

Refer to steps 3 and 4 to carve two symmetrical heart shapes between the adjacent waterdrops made in step 10.

12

Repeat step 11 to complete the remaining five shapes.

13

Carve a waterdrop shape between the adjacent hearts made in step 12.

14

Repeat step 13 to complete the remaining five shapes.

Christmas

Hearts and flowers 2

The combination of heart, conical, and waterdrop shapes looks like crystals of snow.

Difficulty ● ● ● ● ○

Carve six waterdrop shapes in the middle of the side of the apple.

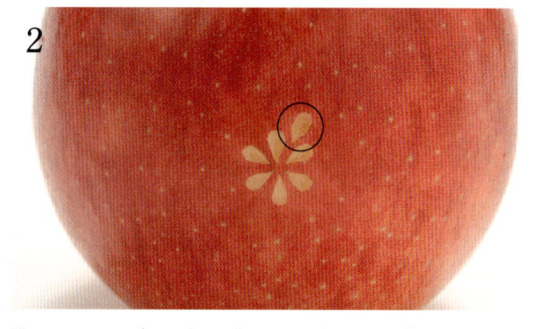

Carve a waterdrop shape between the two adjacent waterdrops made in step 1.

123

3

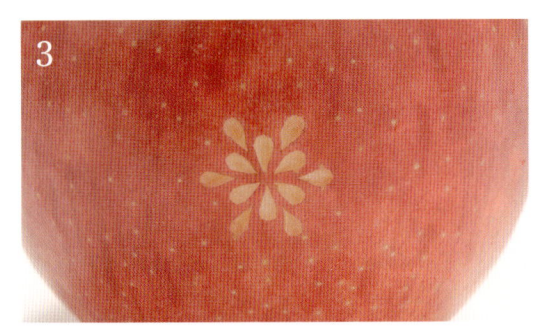

Repeat step 2 to complete the remaining five shapes.

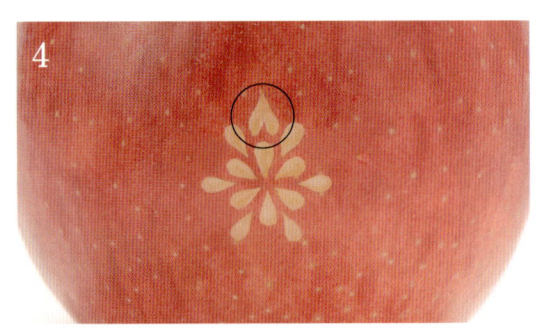

4

Carve an inverted heart shape between the adjacent waterdrops carved in step 3. Cut clockwise from the lower end of the heart, and stop at the center of the top of the heart. Use the same process on the other side. Cut counterclockwise from the lower end of the heart, and stop at the center of the top of the heart.

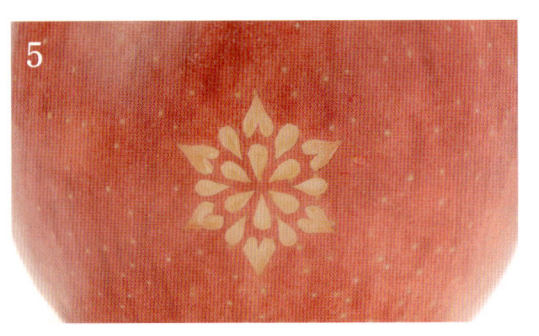

5

Repeat step 4 to complete the remaining five shapes.

6

Carve three waterdrop shapes on the outer side of one of the waterdrops carved in step 3.

7

Repeat step 6 to complete the remaining five shapes.

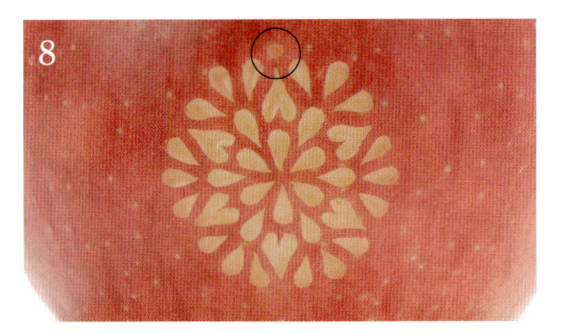

8

Carve a conical shape under one of the hearts carved in step 5.

9

Repeat step 8 to complete the remaining five shapes.

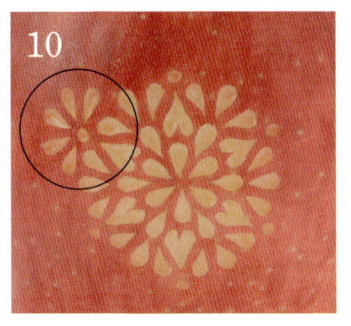

10

Carve five waterdrop shapes around one of the conical shapes carved in step 9.

11

Repeat step 10 to complete the remaining five shapes.

12

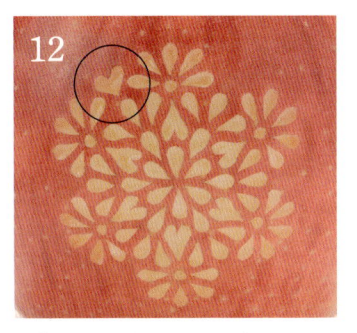

Refer to step 4 to carve a heart shape between two adjacent waterdrops carved in step 11.

13

Repeat step 12 to complete the remaining five shapes.

14

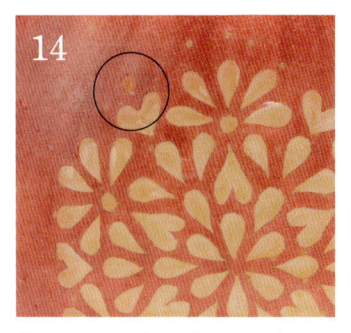

Carve a waterdrop shape on the outer side of one of the hearts carved in step 13.

15

Repeat step 14 to complete the remaining five shapes.

16

Carve five waterdrop shapes on the outer side of one of the waterdrops carved in step 15.

17

Repeat step 16 to complete the remaining five shapes, and the work is completed.

Christmas

Oriental style

Use the tip of the carving knife to draw intricate, detailed patterns.
A step up to master the advanced techniques.

| Difficulty | ● ● ● ● ● |

1 Draw six equally divided marking lines at the top of the apple. Carve six petals 5mm deep based on the marking lines.

2 Carve an arc between the adjacent petals at half the length of the petal. The arc meets the edge of the petal.

126

3

Carve an arc 5mm deep on the outer side of the arc carved in step 2.

4

Carve a "レ"-shaped groove on the outer side of the arc completed in step 3.

5

Using the line in the picture as an example, carve another arc 5mm deep on the outer side of the arc completed in step 4 to connect the top ends of the two petals.

6

Carve a "レ"-shaped groove on the outer side of the arc completed in step 5.

7

Repeat steps 2 through 6 to complete the remaining five shapes.

8

Two large "V" shapes are carved between two adjacent petals.

9. Repeat step 8 to complete the remaining five shapes.

10. Carve two waterdrops arranged like a "/\" shape between the two "V" shapes. The spacing between the waterdrops should be consistent with the spacing between the "V" shapes.

11. Carve a bigger waterdrop between the two waterdrops carved in step 10.

12. Repeat steps 10 and 11 to complete a circle of shapes.

13. Trace the outline of the waterdrops 5mm deep, using the line in the picture as an example. The outline of the lower part of the waterdrop in the middle should have a prominent sharp corner.

14. Carve a "レ"-shaped groove on the outer side of the line carved in step 13.

15. Draw an arc between two adjacent waterdrops, and remove the excess material.

16. Carve a small serrated triangle on the outer side of the arc carved in step 15. Insert the knife tip slightly into the pulp, move the knife diagonally from left to right, change the cutting angle, and move the knife to the upper right-hand side. Repeat this process, and cut consecutively to complete the zigzag line.

17. Carve a "レ"-shaped groove on the outer side of the zigzag line carved in step 16.

18

Remove the excess material, and the zigzag line composed of small triangles is completed.

19

Repeat steps 16 and 17 to complete a total of six rows of zigzag lines.

20

Repeat steps 15 through 19 to complete the entire circle.

21

Carve a large "V" between two adjacent waterdrops.

22

Repeat step 21 to complete the entire circle.

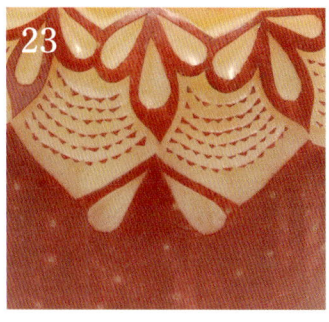

23

Carve two waterdrops arranged in a "/\" shape between two adjacent "V" shapes. The space between the waterdrops should be consistent with the space between the "V" shapes.

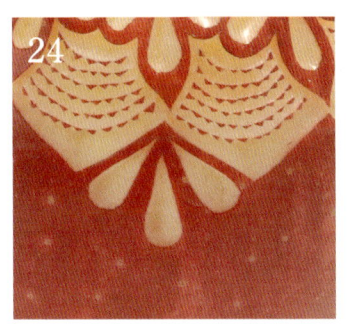

24

Carve a larger waterdrop between the two waterdrops carved in step 23.

25

Repeat steps 23 and 24 to complete the entire circle, and the work is finished.

129

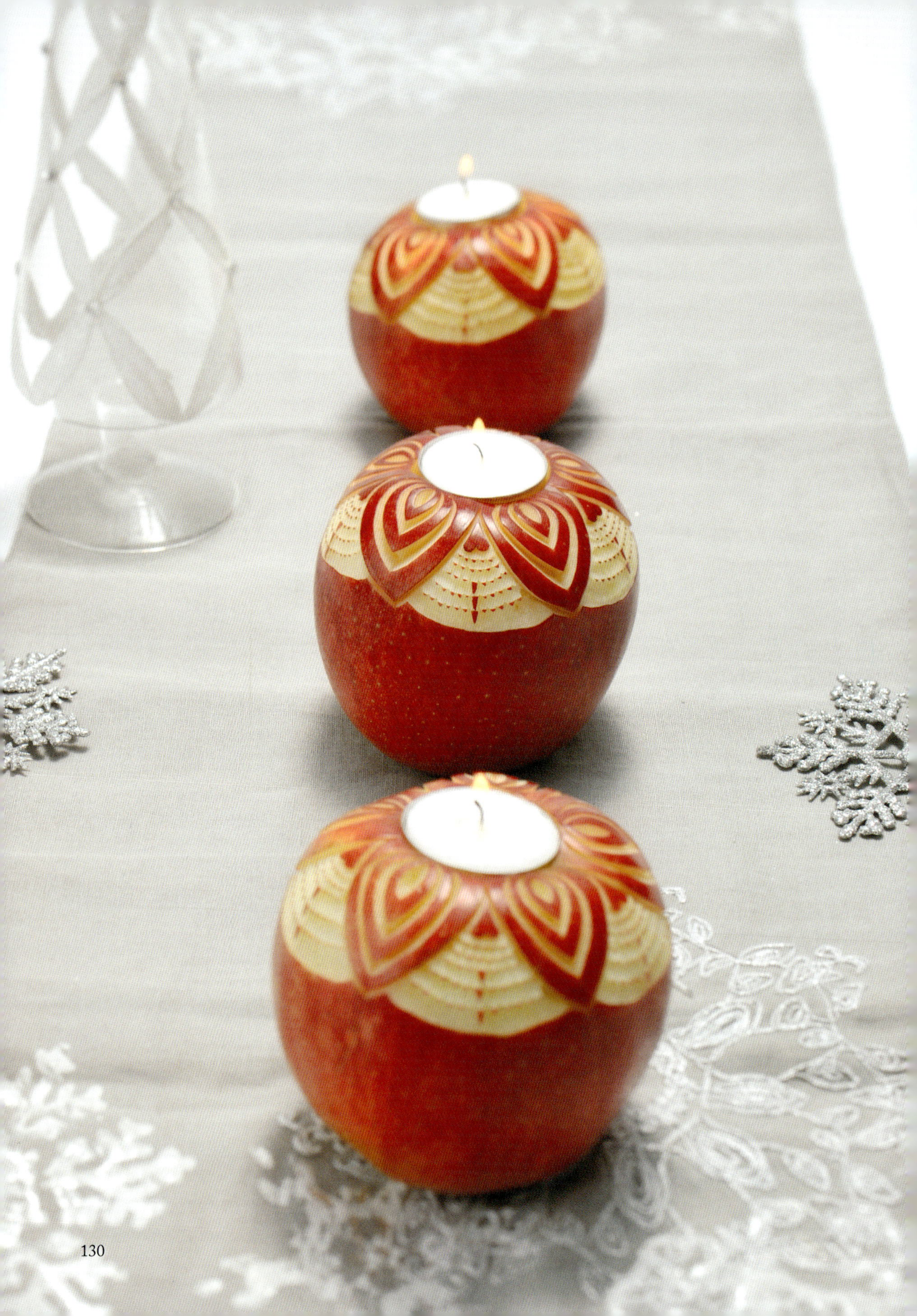

Christmas

Floral design candlestick

A stylish, carved-apple candle stick. Light a candle on Christmas night.

Difficulty ● ● ● ● ●

1

Carve a circle at the top of the apple that is big enough to hold a candle. The carved circle should also be deep enough for the candle.

2

Carve a large "レ" shape inside the circular outline carved in step 1 to make it into a deeper round hole. If the core remains, remove it.

3 As shown in the picture, the depth should be just enough to place a candle in it, with only the wick exposed.

4 Draw five equally separated marking lines extending from the circle.

5 Carve five petals using the lines in the picture as an example.

6 Carve a "レ"-shaped groove on the outer side of the petals carved in step 5.

7 Carve an eye-like shape near the edge of the round hole at the center of the petal.

8 Using the lines in the picture as an example, outline the eye-like shaped with a line 5mm deep.

9 Carve a "レ"-shaped groove on the outer side of the line carved in step 8.

10 Make another outline using the line in the picture as an example.

11 Carve a "レ"-shaped groove on the outer side of the line carved in step 10, and one petal is completed.

132

12 Repeat steps 7 through 11 to complete the remaining four shapes. Carve an inverted heart shape 5mm deep between the two adjacent petals.

13 Carve a "レ"-shaped groove on the outer side of the line carved in step 12, engrave the outside of the carved shapes into semicircular shapes, and remove the excess material.

14 Carve a small serrated triangle on the outer side of the heart. Insert the knife tip slightly into the pulp, move the knife diagonally from left to right, and then, change the cutting angle and move the knife to the upper right-hand side. Repeat this process and cut consecutively to complete the zigzag line.

15 Carve a "レ"-shaped groove on the outer side of the zigzag line carved in step 14.

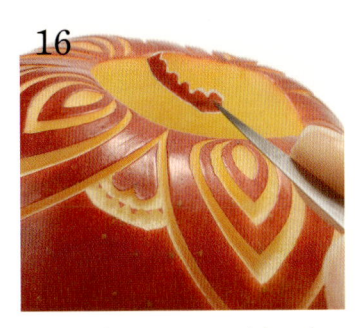

16 Remove the excess material, and the zigzag line created from the small triangles is completed.

17 Repeat steps 14 through 16 to engrave the second row of zigzag lines.

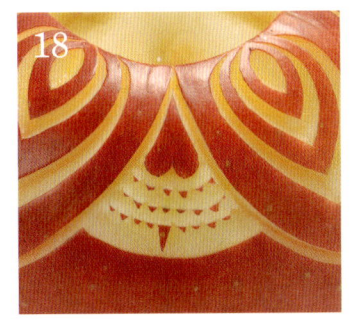

18 The triangle in the middle of the third row should be made a little longer.

19 The triangle in the middle of the fourth and fifth rows should be made a little longer. Repeat steps 12 through 18 to complete the remaining four shapes. Finally, put in the candle, and the work is completed.

133

practical tips
Preserving apple works

If a carved apple is discolored, the appearance of the work will be diminished. The following section introduces effective preservation methods.

Soak the apple in salt water to prevent discoloration

Soak for ten seconds to a maximum of two minutes.
Soak for only a few seconds if the design is complex.

The peel of a carved apple comes off easily, so do not soak it for too long. A quick dip will be enough for pieces with delicate designs. After soaking, wipe gently with a paper towel so that it retains only a little water. Be careful not to remove the peel. Wrap the apple in a plastic wrap and put it into the refrigerator.

How to select apples
If an apple has scars or feels quite soft, it is not suitable for carving. Try to use fresh apples without scars.

Attachment: cherry radish
Carved cherry radishes can also easily lose their peel or become wrinkled. To avoid wrinkling, soak radishes in water for a few seconds. Be careful to avoid soaking for too long, or the radish will swell and peel. As with the apples, dry the radish leaving a little moisture, wrap it in plastic wrap, and put it into the refrigerator.

birthday

Get together with friends and family to celebrate the special day!

birthday
Watermelon birthday party
Celebrate with a watermelon-engraved cake, perfect for birthday parties. Add a dash of color with these adorable designs.

Vegetables and fruits to be used

Watermelons, cherry radishes, colored peppers and parsley

Key tips

Watermelon cake
The white parts of watermelons can be used to imitate ladyfingers and whipped cream. The "V"-shaped carvings made on top of and around the dome should look like the piped decorations of a cake. The "S" shapes that flow from the top of the watermelon recreate whipped cream carefully spread across a cake with a palette knife.

Watermelon balls as accessories
Among the fruits commonly used in fruit and vegetable carving, watermelons are especially suitable because they provide a variety of colors and textures. Many design variations are made by using the change of color from green, white to red. It is possible to make hearts with watermelon peel, dig out the flesh in the shape of small balls, and make various accessories.

Cherry radish
Cherry radishes have a sharp contrast of red and white. Although they are small in size, it can be used to make vivid works. When carving cherry radishes, the carving must be accurate to the millimeter. When carving its skin, try to keep the spacing consistent to ensure accuracy. However, caution is required as cherry radishes peel easily.

Colored pepper bowl
The cherry radishes are displayed on small bowls made with colored peppers. The edge of the bowl can also be jagged. When a cherry radish and some parsley on the colored pepper bowl are displayed in a dish, the rich and pleasant colors would surely make the atmosphere of a birthday party even more exciting.

birthday

Happy birthday lettering

A gorgeous watermelon sculpture to make a birthday party even more lovely.

Difficulty ● ● ● ● ●

1

Place the watermelon on its side, and draw a circle using the line in the picture as an example. Paste the paper stencils to match the curve of the circle.

2

Insert the knife through the paper stencil and carve the letters holding the knife perpendicular to the watermelon. If the letter has a hollow center, cut the hollow center first. Cut a "レ"-shaped groove from outside the letter. As in the picture, remove all the peel from inside the circle and around the lettering, then draw twenty-four evenly spaced markers around the circle.

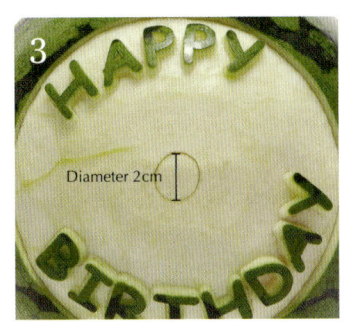

3. Draw a small circle in the middle of the large circle with a diameter of 2cm and a depth of 1cm.

4. Cut slantwise inside the small circle drawn in step 3, and remove the pulp while carving.

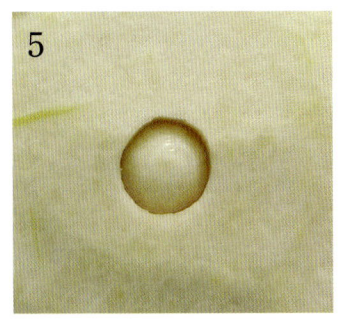

5. Smooth the sharp areas and make them round. A dome shape is completed.

6. Cut slantwise on the outer side of the dome shape and remove a circle of pulp.

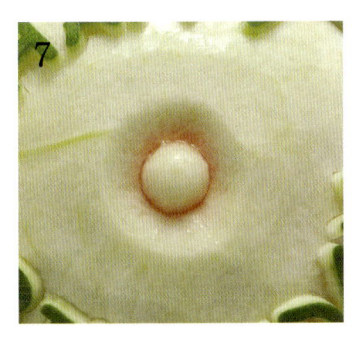

7. This is how it looks after removing the pulp.

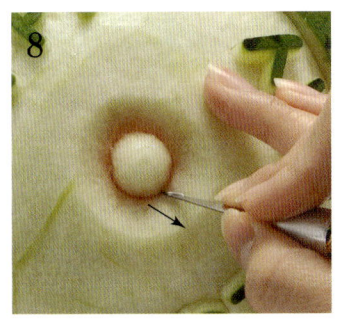

8. Next, carve the center of the gerbera. Carve a circle of small triangles around the dome shape, moving the knife diagonally from left to right.

9. Change the angle while keeping the knife in the fruit, and cut to the upper right-hand side to complete the triangle. Each triangular petal shape is carved in one stroke.

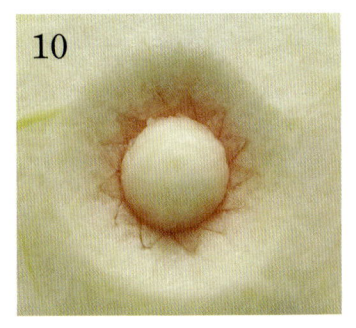

10. Repeat steps 8 and 9 to complete the whole circle.

11. Shave the area below the outer side of the triangles to highlight the triangles.

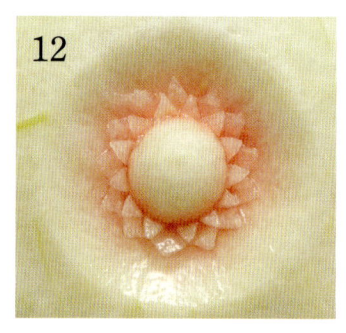

12 Refer to steps 8 through 10 to carve triangles between adjacent triangles of the first row. Shave the area below the outer side of the triangles to highlight the triangles.

13 Smooth the sharp areas and make them round.

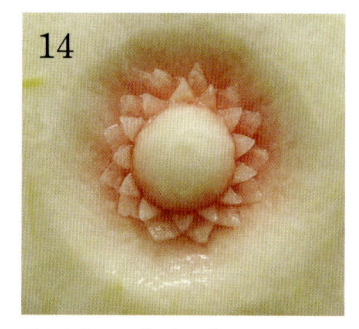

14 This is how it looks after trimming.

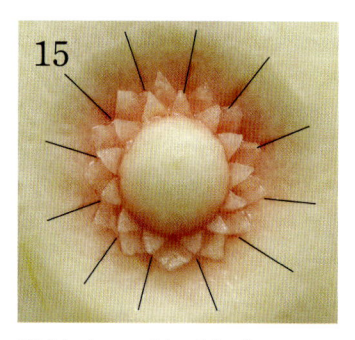

15 Divide the outside of the flower center into twelve equal parts.

16 Carve first the left, then the right side of the petal using the lines as markers.

17 Carve the outline of twelve petals.

18 Shave the area below the outer side of the petals to highlight the petals.

19 Trim the sharp areas of the petals to make them smooth.

20 Trim all twelve petals.

21

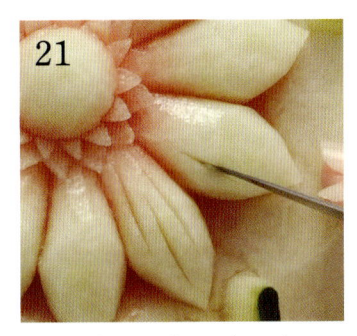

Carve a few small "V"-shaped grooves into the petals.

22

This is how it looks after the twelve petals are finished. The gerbera is completed.

23

Make the outside pattern. Carve "V"-shaped grooves on the markers made in step 2, first cutting diagonally from left to right, then diagonally from right to left, completing "V" shapes with a gentle slope.

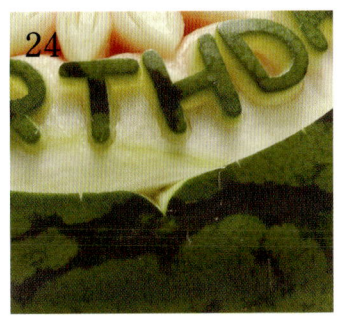

24

This is how it looks after removing the excess material.

25

Repeat step 23 to complete the whole circle.

26

Trim the pattern finished in step 25 and the gerbera to make everything smooth.

27

Next, carve twelve bows. Carve sideways waterdrops under the arcs between the "V" shapes. To make the carving easier, move the watermelon and the knife simultaneously in opposite directions.

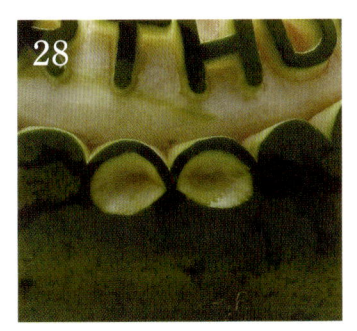

28

A drop shape is also carved in the adjacent position to form a pair of waterdrops.

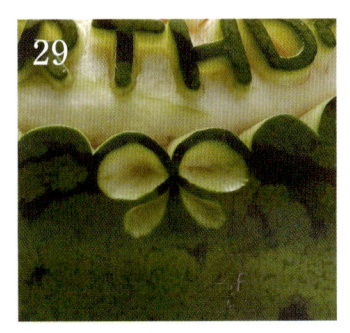

29

Carve two small symmetrical waterdrops below them. A bow shape is completed.

141

30 Repeat steps 27 through 29 to complete the circle. Twelve bows are completed.

31 Outline the row of bows by carving out a "レ"-shaped groove around them.

32 Repeat step 31 to complete the circle.

33 Make semicircles below the bows by carving arcs while holding the knife at an angle.

34 This is how it looks after removing the excess material.

35 Repeat step 33 to complete the circle.

36 Outline the semicircles by carving a row of arcs while holding the knife at an angle to create a new row of semicircles.

37 Repeat step 36 to complete the circle. The work is finished.

38 This is the completed piece looked at from the top.

birthday

Lined hearts

Make lined hearts with red fruits to enhance the lovely atmosphere of the party.

Difficulty ● ○ ○ ○ ○

1

About 3mm

Cut an apple into a heart shape. Insert the knife vertically at the position about 3mm from the edge of the heart shape, and carve a small heart shape 3mm deep.

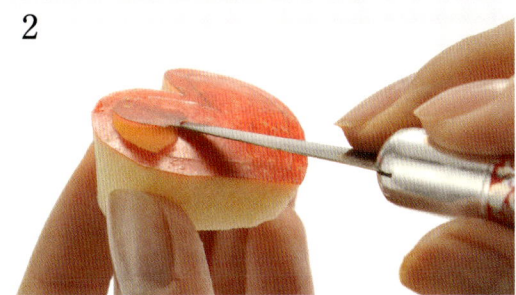

2

Carve "レ"-shaped grooves from the inside towards the line carved in step 1.

3

Repeat step 2 to complete a peel-rimmed heart.

4

String together the heart-shaped apples and strawberries, and the work is completed.

birthday

Watermelon cake

A striking watermelon cake, elaborately carved.

Difficulty ● ● ● ○ ○

1. Cut a watermelon in half. Draw a row of semicircular arcs on the peel using the lines in the picture as an example.

2. Carve 5mm deep along the lines in step 1.

3. Carve a "レ"-shaped groove from the bottom towards the line carved in step 2.

4. This is how it looks after removing the excess material.

5. Repeat step 4 to complete the circle.

6. Carve three waterdrop shapes on the inner side of the arc.

7. Repeat step 6 to complete the circle.

8. Shave off the peel, leaving just the inner area of the arc with the waterdrop shapes.

9. This is how it looks after shaving the entire peel.

10 Carve a circle 1cm deep, about 4cm below the waterdrop shapes.

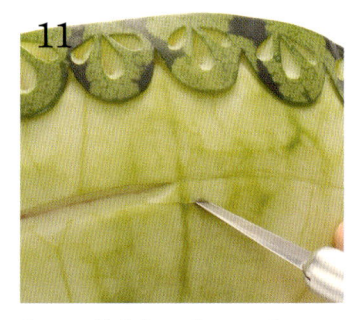

11 Carve a "レ"-shaped groove from the bottom towards the line carved in step 10.

12 Repeat step 11 to complete the circle.

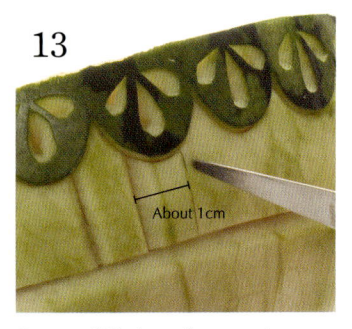

13 Carve a "V"-shaped groove 1cm deep between the waterdrop shape and the line carved in step 10. The distance between two adjacent "V"-shaped grooves should be 1cm.

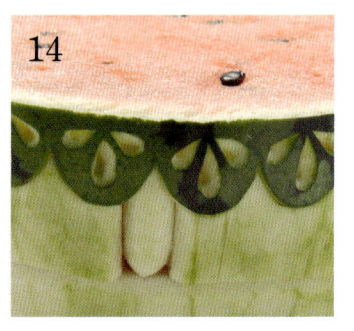

14 Trim the cuts and tips smooth, and make this into the shape of a sponge finger.

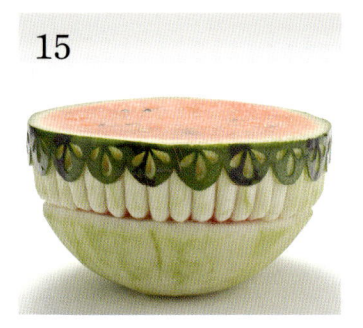

15 Repeat steps 13 and 14 to complete the circle.

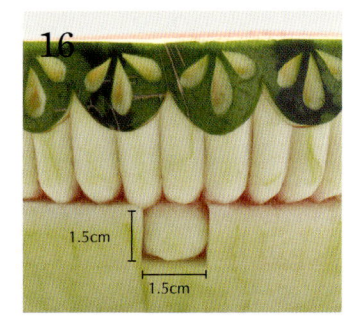

16 Complete a circle 1.5cm below the sponge-finger shape. Then, carve a square between the new line and the line below the sponge-finger shape that has a length and width of 1.5cm and a depth of 1cm. Trim the square smooth to create a dome.

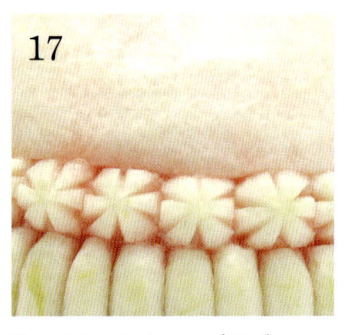

17 Repeat step 16 to complete the row of domes. Carve six "V" shapes from the center of the domes outward, to make a row of what looks like piping decoration of whipped cream.

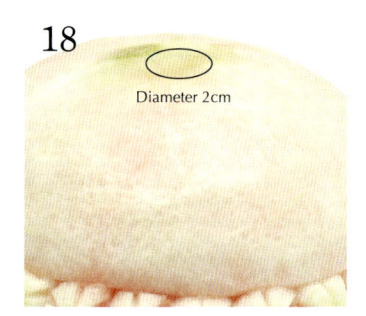

18 Draw a circle with a diameter of 2cm at the top of the watermelon.

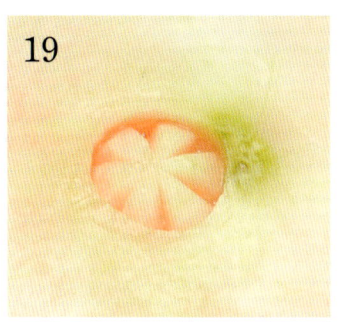

19 Remove the internal pulp, and make it into a small dome shape. Similar to step 17, carve "V"-shaped grooves on it, to make it look like whipped cream.

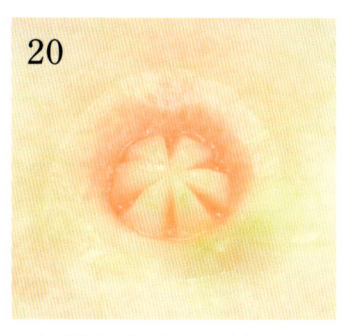

20 To highlight the shape of the cream, shave the outside of the circle to widen it, and then trim the rough areas to make them round.

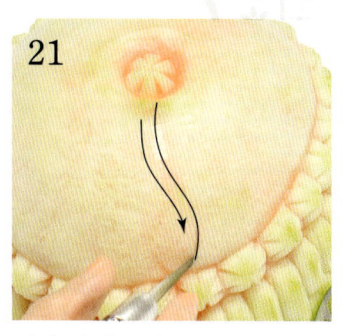

21 Tilt the knife and carve an "S"-shaped line 1.5cm deep.

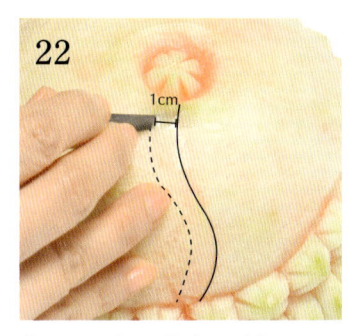

22 Carve another "S"-shaped line 1cm away from the "S"-shaped line that carved in step 21 with the knife tilted even more.

23 This is how it looks after removing the excess material.

24 Repeat steps 21 and 22 to complete a circle of "S" shapes.

25 Place the heart shapes made out of watermelon peel on top as decorations, and the work is completed.

birthday

Watermelon bowls

Cut a watermelon in half to make these lovely watermelon bowls!

| Difficulty | ● ○ ○ ○ ○ |

1 Cut the watermelon in half.

2 Scoop out the pulp with a melon baller.

3 Scoop as much as possible, then remove the remainder with a knife to clean the inside.

4

Use a spoon to clean out the places that cannot be reached with the knife.

5

This is how it looks after removing all the pulp.

6

Divide the edge of the peel into twelve equal parts, and carve a marking line that is about 1cm long. Carve diagonally from left to right, then from right to left towards the marking line. The two cuts join and form a smooth "V" shape.

7

This is how it looks after removing the excess material.

8

Repeat step 6 to complete the circle.

9

Carve a heart shape between two adjacent "V" shapes.

10

This is how it looks after hollowing out and removing the excess material.

11

Repeat step 9 to complete the circle.

12

Place the pulp balls scooped out in step 2, the hearts carved in step 9, and some mint leaves in the bowl as decoration, and the work is completed.

149

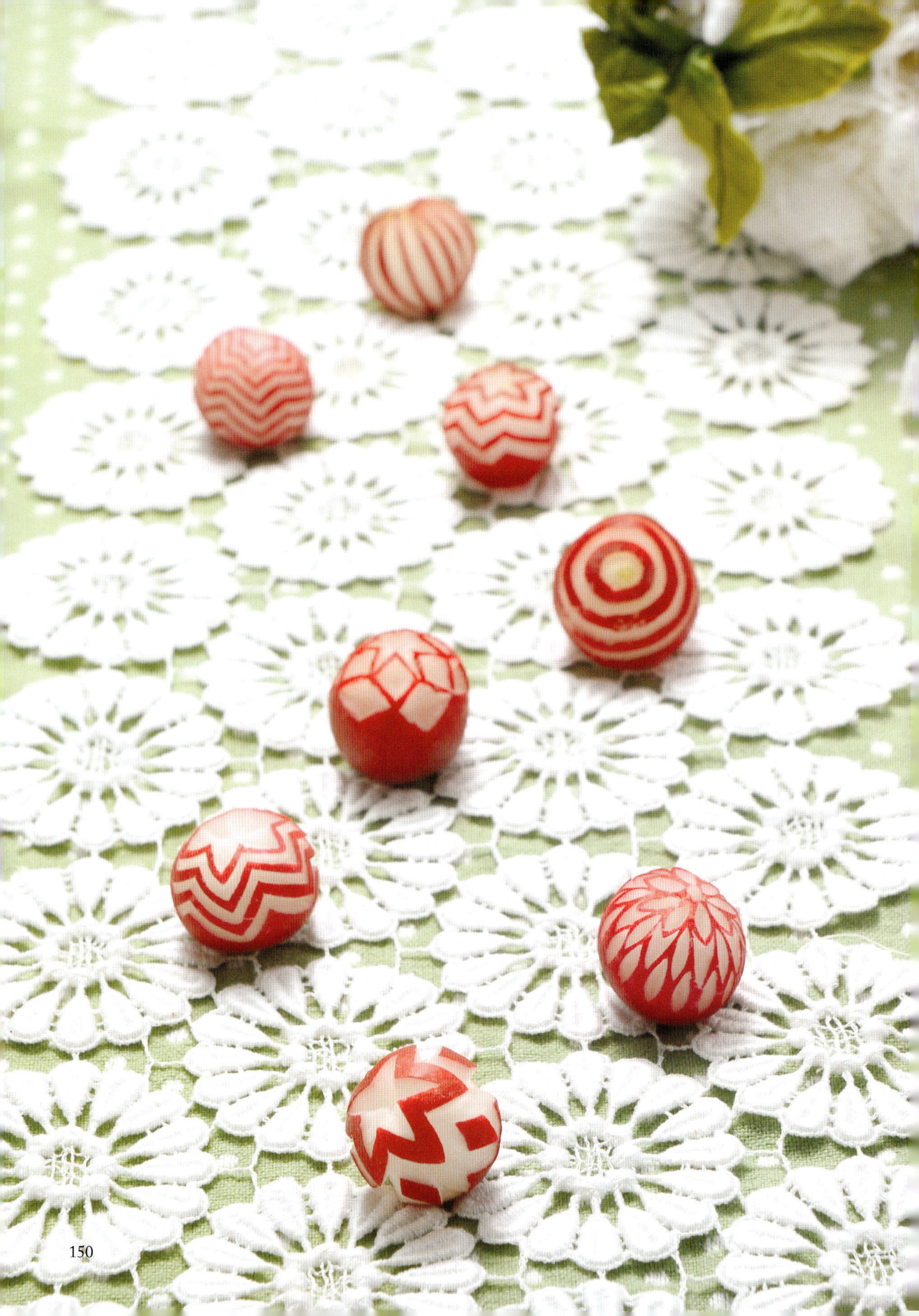

birthday

Various cherry radish works

Cherry radishes with different designs to liven up any decoration.

| Difficulty | ● ● ○ ○ ○ |

1

Cut away the tip and root of the cherry radish.

2

Cut the root to show a bit of the white flesh.

3

Cherry radish 1: Insert the knife so it is perpendicular to the radish, and carve a circle 3 mm deep. Carve a "レ"-shaped groove towards the the circle.

4

This is how it looks after carving the groove.

151

5

Repeat step 3 to carve the second circle, the third circle, and so on. Then, the piece is completed.

6

Cherry radish 2: Apply the same process in steps 1 and 2, and then carve a "V"-shaped groove from the top down.

7

Carve another one on the opposite side of the "V" groove in step 6.

8

Repeat step 6 to complete the circle.

9

Cherry radish 3: Apply the process in steps 1 and 2, trace the outline of a star, tilt the knife, and then cut from the sides towards the center. Remove the excess material.

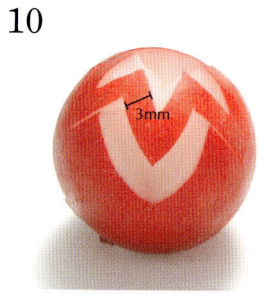

10

Outline the star by carving a line outside it, leaving 3mm in between. Carve a "レ"-shaped groove from the second line towards the star.

11

Repeat step 10 to complete the remaining four shapes.

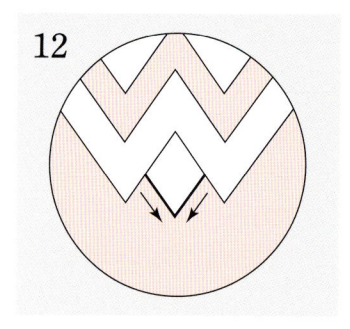

12

As shown in the picture, carve a diamond between two adjacent points of the star.

13

Carve a "レ"-shaped groove towards the line carved in step 12.

14

This is how it looks after the diamond is carved out.

15

Repeat steps 12 and 13 to complete the remaining four shapes, and the work is completed.

16

Cherry radish 4: Apply the same process in steps 1 and 2. Make six incisions from the center, 5mm deep.

17

Carve a "レ"-shaped groove on each side of the line carved in step 16.

18

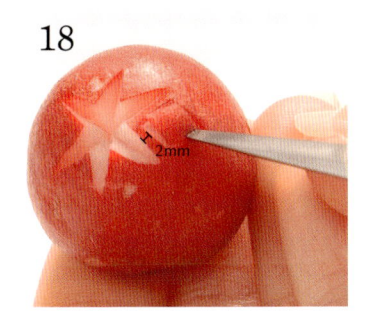

Carve a square pyramid between two adjacent edges, leaving 2mm between shapes. Each square pyramid should be 5mm deep.

19

This is how it looks after carving four sides. Remove the excess material.

20

Repeat steps 18 and 19 to complete the remaining five shapes.

21

In the same way, and leaving a width of about 2mm, carve a larger square pyramid between the two adjacent square pyramids that were carved in step 20. After the whole circle is completed, the work is finished.

22

Cherry radish 5: Apply the same process in steps 1 and 2. Make six incisions, 5mm deep, that meet in the center. Carve eye-like shapes on each line.

23 Repeat step 22 to complete the remaining five shapes.

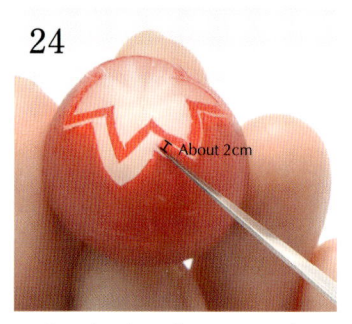

24 Outline the shape by carving a line 3mm deep, leaving 2mm of space, then carve "レ"-shaped grooves towards the line

25 Repeat step 24 to complete the whole circle.

26 Repeat step 24 to complete the second circle, the third circle, and so on until the whole work is finished.

27 **Cherry radish 6:** Apply the same process in steps 1 and 2. Make eight incisions, 5mm deep, using the line in picture as an example. Carve an eye-like shape on each marking line.

28 Repeat step 27, and the eight petals are completed.

29 Continue to carve the second circle of eye-like shapes slightly below the middle of the adjacent petals of the first circle. Between the two eye-like shapes of the second circle, using the petal of the first circle as the model, carve two slash-like strokes, and then carve an eye-like shape under the slashes.

30 Repeat step 29 to complete the whole circle, and the second circle is completed.

31 Continue to carve the eye-like shapes slightly below the middle of the adjacent petals of the second circle. After the circle is completed, the work is finished.

154

birthday

Zucchini boat-shaped plate

Carve freely on the zucchini shape to create a unique, one-and-only plate.

Difficulty ● ○ ○ ○ ○

1

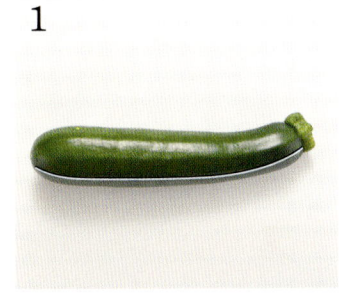

Cut the zucchini vertically, and divide it half.

2

This is a cross section of the cut.

3

If the zucchini does not stand properly, shave a bit of the bottom to make it stable.

4

Draw several curves, and carve a "V"-shaped groove on each curve.

5

Carve several eye-like shapes outside of the curve.

6

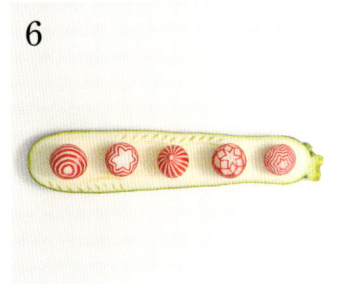

Place the cherry radish works on it, and the work is completed.

birthday

Colored pepper dish

The bright color of peppers can set off the beauty of cherry radish works.

| Difficulty | ● ○ ○ ○ ○ |

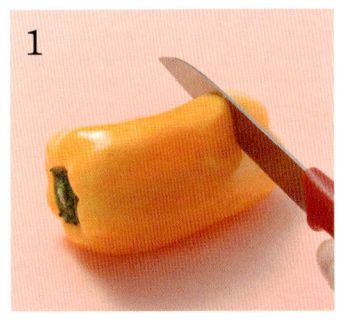

1 Cut a length of 2cm from the bottom of the pepper without the pedicle. The remaining part can be used for carving pepper tulips (see p. 72).

2 This is the cross section.

3 Cut out the internal parts that are connected together to make room for the works of cherry radishes.

4 Clean the interior well.

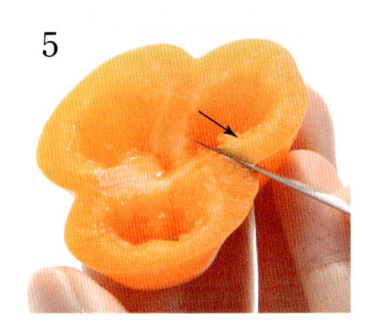

5 Carve a zigzag line on the edge, tilting the knife and cutting from the upper left-hand side to the lower right-hand side.

6 Follow the a zigzag line cut in step 5, and continue to cut slantwise from the upper right-hand side to the lower left-hand side.

7 Now a sawtooth effect is completed. For aesthetic reasons, try to keep the cutting angle, width, and size of the left cut consistent with those of the right cut.

8 Repeat steps 5 and 6 to complete the whole circle, and the serrated lace is completed.

9 Put works made from cherry radishes and some parsley in the pepper dish, and the work is completed.

art exhibition

The charm of carving

Finger-food style carvings
Distribute carved vegetables together with crackers to your guests. The picture shows radishes on a bell pepper dish, but they can be used to hold potato salad as well.

Apple hearts
Entertain guests with these small, engraved hearts to turn any visit into a success. Very red apples, such as Jonagold or Ruby Sweet are recommended.

art exhibition

Ingenious seasonal design

Apple christmas tree and apple santa claus
How about a Christmas display made from just one apple? Line up trees made from apples on a white plate and the effect is complete.

Butternut squash Halloween
Carve deep into the butternut squash and expose the orange inside for maximum impact. Butternut squash is recommended for carving, as they are easier to preserve than Halloween pumpkins. It is recommended to use butternut squash for carving, which is easier to preserve than a Halloween pumpkin.

wedding

Decorate weddings with exquisitely engraved watermelons to commemorate these once-in-a-lifetime events of happiness.

wedding
The beauty of blessing
An astounding assemblage of extravagantly sculpted artwork.
Sure to mesmerize all wedding guests, it will forever be remembered together with the memories of this lifetime event.

Vegetables and fruits to be used
Watermelons

Key tips

Color
The exposed parts of the red pulp of each work are all different. On the lower left-hand side is a silhouette of the bride, around which the color is slightly flushed as though the bride is being embraced. On the upper left-hand side is a fan-themed piece, with a deepening gradation of red. When arranging the overall display, pay attention to the balance of red in each work.

Candle
Lighting candles in a dimly lit space makes the atmosphere elegant and romantic. The glass is filled with water, with a dreamy candle floating on it. The candlelight sways. It is fantastic. It is different than the effect displayed in bright light, with a really special flavor.

Transparent tubular vase
Tranparent tubes are ideal for adding height to the display without interfering with the final effect. They can also be used to add depth and make the entire display grand. Place the watermelons facing slightly diagonally so that the intricate designs on the sides can also be seen.

Ensemble
Place the tallest vase, with a large bouquet of flowers, in the rear. Use white flowers in the center to match the bride's bouquet and for a lustrous effect. The green of the leaves and the watermelons spread to unite the display as one art piece. Add a white butterfly made from paper, and it is simply a fairytale kingdom.

Other scenes at the wedding

At the center of the venue, there is a large, live tree decorated with several watermelon carvings among the tree's lush green foliage. Candles placed around the watermelons and hung from the branches create a fairytale world with their swaying candlelight. It is a reception area ripe with artistry and skill.

161

wedding
Rose welcome decoration
Decorate the reception area to greet guests with a sense of exclusivity.

Vegetables and fruits to be used

Watermelons

Key tips

Welcome
The "Welcome" engraving of the watermelon is perfect to decorate the reception area of a wedding. Large and small bows surround the lettering and the roses, and the carved hearts and skillfully crafted lace combine to make a charming and feminie design.

Names and date
The piece engraved with the bride and groom's names and wedding date blesses the newlywed's special day. To maintain the unity of the overall design, the peel is patterned with four eye-like shapes, and the red pulp is intricately carved into a rose.

Roses
If the reception area is limited, a watermelon piece engraved "Welcome" and another decorated with the bride and groom's names and the wedding date would be sufficient to decorate it. The green emphasised in one work and the red accentuated in the other create a stark contrast, but the roses on both pieces bring out a sense of harmony.

Small accessories
Additional decorations should be coordinated in simple whites and greens to blend in with the green of the watermelons and to bring out the red of the roses. The flowers, candles, birds and rabbits are all matched in white. The freshness and softness of this display is perfect for outdoor weddings as well.

wedding

Big rose

A large rose in full bloom! Master this rose design which is used in other works as well.

| Difficulty | ● ● ● ● ○ |

1

Place the watermelon on its side, and draw a circle that will become the core of the rose. Use the lines in the above picture as an example. The size of the circle should be about the radius of the watermelon. Hold the knife vertically and cut along the circle to a depth of 2cm.

2

Carve a "レ"-shaped groove on the inner side of the circle carved in step 1.

3

Widen the circle carved in step 1 by carving its outside while keeping the knife held at an angle.

4

Carve the first petal. Cut on the edge of the inside of the flower core along the lines shown in the picture.

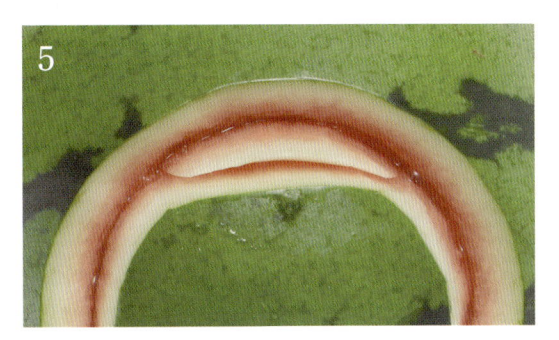

5

Slice off the peel from the area of the flower core that is opposite the line cut in step 4 while carving sideways with the knife, to highlight the petal.

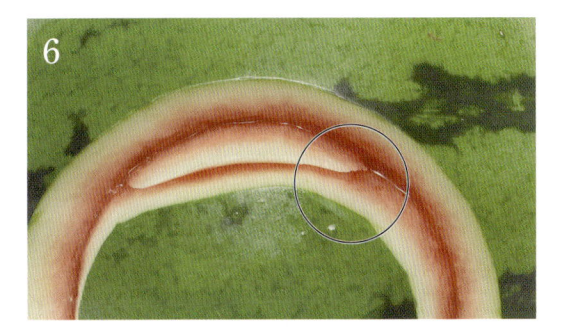

6

Because the second petal will be on the right-hand side of the first one, it is necessary to round the area shown in the picture.

7

The second petal should overlap a bit with the first one. Cut on the edge of the inside of the flower core along the lines shown in the picture.

8

Slice off the peel from the area of the flower core that is opposite the line cut in step 7 while carving sideways with the knife, to highlight the petal.

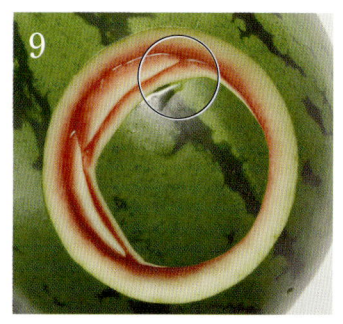

9 Because the third petal will be on the right-hand side of the first one, it is necessary to round the area shown in the picture.

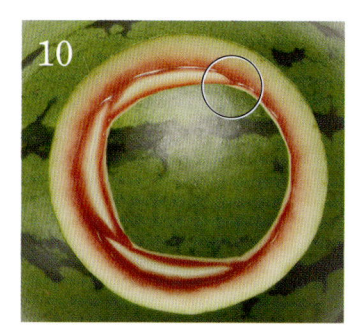

10 Repeat the same process to complete the third petal. Because the fourth petal will be on the right-hand side of the first one, it is necessary to round the area shown in the picture.

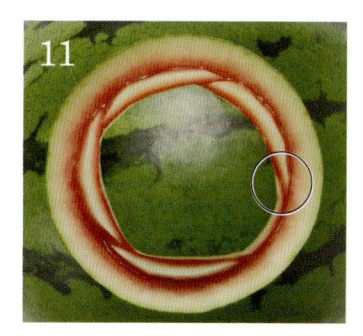

11 Repeat the same process to complete the fourth petal. Because the fifth petal will be on the right-hand side of the first one, it is necessary to round the area shown in the picture.

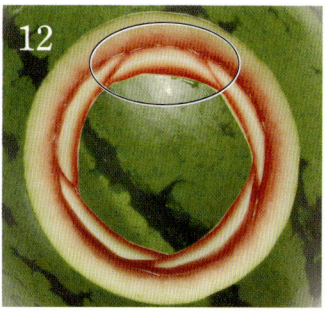

12 Repeat the same process to complete the fifth petal. The fifth petal should come slightly under the first one.

13 Cut the inner edge and carve an angle to the interior of the flower core. Remove the peel from the flower core.

14 Next, make the first petal of the second layer. Using the line in the picture as an example, cut along the inner side of the flower core, from roughly the middle of one of the petals in the first layer to a point slightly passing the middle of the petal on its right.

15 Cut slantwise on the inner side of the line cut in step 14 to highlight the petal.

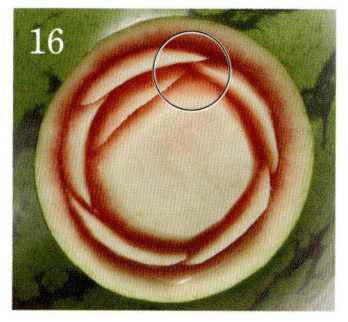

16 Because the second petal will be on the right-hand side of the first one, it is necessary to round the area shown in the picture.

17 The second petal should overlap a bit with the first one. Cut on the edge of the inside of the flower core along the lines shown in the picture.

166

18 Cut slantwise on the inner side of the line cut in step 17 to highlight the petal. Because the third petal will be on the right-hand side of the first one, it is necessary to round the area shown in the picture.

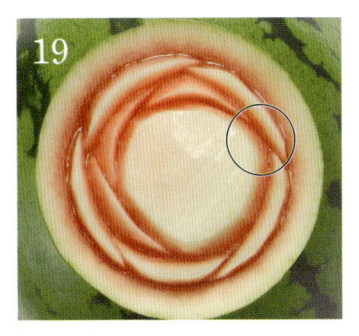

19 Repeat the same process to complete the third petal. Because the fourth petal will be on the right-hand side of the third one, it is necessary to round the area shown in the picture.

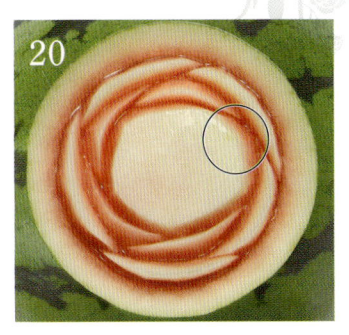

20 Repeat the same process to complete the fourth petal. Because the fifth petal will be on the right-hand side of the fourth one, it is necessary to round the area shown in the picture.

21 Repeat the same process to complete the fifth petal. The fifth petal should come slightly under, the first one.

22 Slightly carve the inner part of the flower so it becomes angular.

23 This is a slantwise view of the work.

24 Repeat the same process to complete the third layer of petals.

25 Repeat the same process to complete the fourth layer of petals.

26 Repeat the same process to complete the fifth layer of petals.

167

27

This is a slantwise view of the work. Keep carving meticulously inward.

28

Next, form the outer petals. A base cut will be made to add roundness to inside of the petals. Carve a smooth, circular arc, starting from the middle of one of the petals from the first layer and ending around the middle of the petal to its right. When digging the area around the peel outside the circle, be careful not to increase the depth of the flower core.

29

Carve the first petal where the base cut was made, using the line in the picture above as an example.

30

Make a large cut outward from the base cut along the outside of the line carved in step 29.

31

This is how it looks after cutting.

32

Carve another base cut for the second petal.

33

The second petal should slightly overlap with the first one. Make an incision using the line in the picture as an example.

34

Make a large cut outward from the base cut along the outside of the line carved in step 33.

35 This is how it looks after cutting.

36 Carve the third petal in the same way.

37 Carve the fourth petal in the same way.

38 Carve the fifth petal in the same way. The fifth petal should slightly overlap with the end of the first petal.

39 Next, carve the first petal of the second outer layer. First, cut two hill shapes which makes the base cut. Starting from the middle of one of the petals in the first layer and ending around the middle of the petal to its right, carve two hills so that the valley comes right where the two petals in the first layer meet. When digging around the outside of the circle, be careful not to increase the depth of the flower core.

40 Carve a pit in the middle of the two hills to complete the base cut.

41 Carve the first petal on the base cut, adding a pointed edge where the pit was carved.

42 Make a large cut outward from the base cut along the outside of the line carved in step 41.

43 This is how it looks after cutting.

44 Repeat steps 39 and 40 and carve the base cut for the second petal.

45 Carve the second petal, which should slightly overlap with the first one. Carve where the base cut was made, adding a pointed edge where the pit was carved.

46 Make a large cut outward from the base cut along the outside of the line carved in step 45.

47 This is how it looks after cutting.

48 Carve the third petal in the same way.

49 Carve the fourth petal in the same way.

50 Carve the fifth petal in the same way. The fifth petal should slightly overlap with the end of the first petal.

51 Next, carve the first petal of the third outer layer. Pay attention to the angle of the watermelon, and cut a bit more outward as though the petals were stretching outward. Repeat steps 39 and 40 to make the base cut.

170

52 Carve the first petal where the base cut was made, adding a pointed edge where the pit was carved.

53 Make a large cut outward from the base cut along the outside of the line carved in step 52.

54 Repeat steps 51 through 53 to complete the five petals. The fifth petal should slightly overlap with the end of the first petal.

55 This is the how it looks from the side.

56 Next, carve the first petal of the fourth outer layer. Pay attention to the angle of the watermelon, and cut more outward than the third layer, as though the petals are widening even more. Repeat steps 39 and 40 to make the base cut.

57 Carve the first petal where the base cut was made, adding a pointed edge where the pit was carved.

58 Make a large cut outward from the base cut along the outside of the line carved in step 57.

59 Repeat steps 56 through 58 to complete the five petals. The fifth petal should slightly overlap with the end of the first petal.

60 This is how it looks from a side view when all the petals are completed.

61 This is how it looks from the side.

62 Smoothen and flatten the area around the petals.

63 Carve a "V"-shaped groove on the surface smoothened in step 62. Cut diagonally from left to right, in the space between petals.

64 Cut diagonally from right to left to complete the cut made in step 63.

65 This is how it looks after removing the excess material.

66 Carve a "V"-shaped groove on each side of the "V"-shaped groove carved out in step 65, leaving a little space in between. These three grooves make one set of "V" shapes.

67 Carve a set of "V"-shaped grooves at each of the remaining four areas, and the piece is complete.

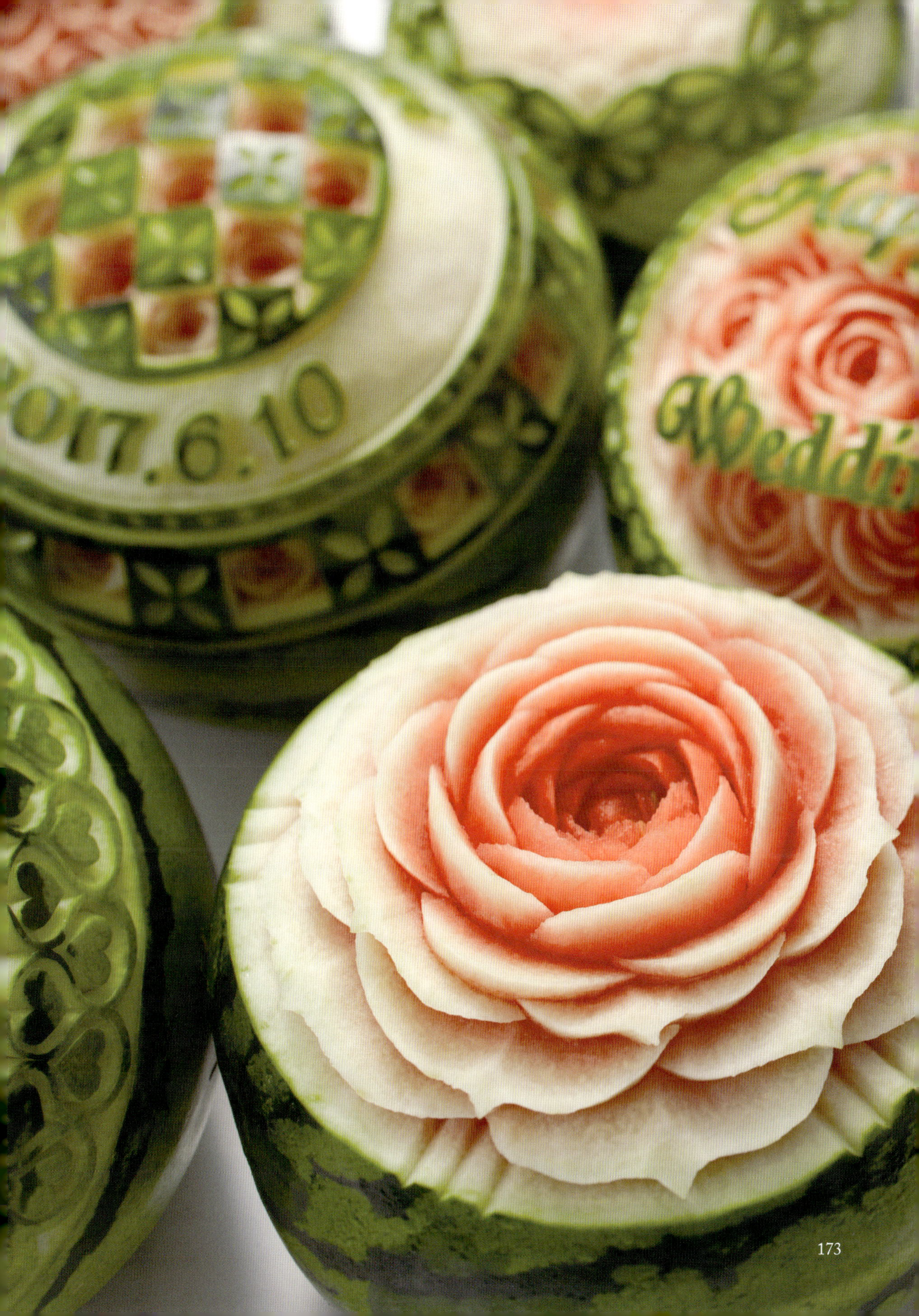
017.6.10
Weddi

wedding

Happy wedding watermelon

The words of blessing, "Happy Wedding" engraved on a romantic, blossoming rose.

| Difficulty | ● ● ● ● ○ |

1
Place the watermelon on its side and paste a paper stencil on it. Follow the illustrated line, and draw a large circle around the stencil. Cut along the circle.

2
Insert the knife through the paper stencil and carve the letters holding the knife perpendicular to the watermelon. If there is a hollow space in the middle of a letter, start carving from the hollow part first, and then carve a "レ"-shaped groove on the outside of the letter. Remove the peel between the carved circle and the letter in step 1, and carve another circle 2cm away from the outside of the first one.

3

Mark a marking line every 1cm on the circle.

4

Carve a "V" shape on each of the marking lines made in step 3. First cut diagonally from left to right, then diagonally from right to left. After doing this on all the marking lines on the circle, the side curves of the adjacent hearts are completed.

5

Carve a "V" shape in the middle of each curve carved in step 4. First cut diagonally from left to right, then diagonally from right to left. After you have carved the entire circle, the curves of the hearts are completed.

6

Carve a heart 1mm away from the edge line on the outer side. Starting from the center of the heart, carve the left half of the heart first.

7

Then carve the right half of the heart, also 1mm from the edge line.

8

This is how it looks after removing the excess material.

9

Repeat steps 6 and 7 to carve a circle of hearts around the melon.

10

Outline the hearts using the line in the picture as an example.

11

Carve a "レ"-shaped groove on the outer side of the edge line carved in step 10.

175

12. Carve the contour line of an inverted heart at the lower end of two adjacent hearts.

13. Remove the peel around the inverted heart carved in step 12 to highlight the three-dimensionality of the heart.

14. Carve a circle farther down.

15. Remove the peel between the inverted heart and the circle carved in step 14.

16. Trim smooth after peeling.

17. Cut slantwise in the area that was peeled in step 16 to carve a smooth "S" shape.

18. Cut slantwise in front of the "S" shape carved in step 17 to shave the lower part of it.

19. This is how it looks after removing the excess material.

20. Repeat steps 17 through 19 to complete the whole circle. To maintain the aesthetic appearance of the "S" shape, care should be taken to keep its angle and width consistent.

21

Carve a rose (see p. 164, "big rose") at the center of the blank space between "Happy" and "Wedding." Then, carve another rose next to it. The center of that rose should slightly overlap with the rose at the center. Note that in order not to affect the lettering, you should not carve the pulp below the words. The key is to cut along the outline of the words and bring out the effect of the connected petals.

22

The tip mentioned in step 21 is shown in the picture. The pulp below each letter is completely preserved, and the word is not affected at all.

23

Carve another rose on the right-hand side of the rose carved in step 21. The petals of the two roses should overlap with each other.

24

Carve another rose on the left-hand side of the rose carved in step 21. The petals of the two roses should overlap with each other.

25

Carve two roses below the word "Wedding" in the same way.

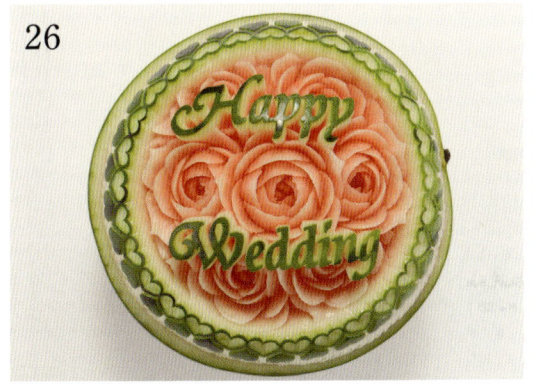

26

Carve two roses above "Happy" to create a flowery effect, and the work is completed.

wedding

Initials of first names

Carve the initials of the names of the bride and the groom on the watermelon to create a unique piece of art.

Difficulty ● ● ● ● ●

1 Place the watermelon on its side and trace a large circle that is based on the illustrated line. The line should be traced lightly because you need to carve a heart here afterward. Paste stencils with the initials on the upper right-hand side of the circle.

2 Insert the knife through the paper stencil and carve the letters holding the knife perpendicular to the watermelon. If there is a hollow place within a letter, start carving from the hollow part. Then, carve a "レ" -shaped groove on the outer side of the letter.

178

3

Remove the peel inside the circle except for the parts of the heart shapes on the circle. Then, trace the outline of the heart.

4

Next, carve the heart. Just as with the carving of a waterdrop shape, move the knife counterclockwise to carve ½ of the heart.

5

Move the knife clockwise to carve the other half of the heart.

6

This is how it looks after removing the excess material.

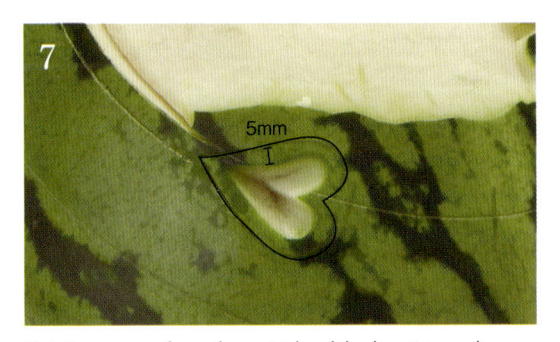

7

Cut 5mm away from the outside of the heart to outline the heart.

8

Carve a "レ"-shaped groove on the outer side of the contour line carved in step 7.

179

9

This is how it looks after removing the excess material.

10

Repeat steps 4 through 8 to engrave three hearts on the left side and five on the right side.

11

At the position 5mm away from the outside of the circle where the peel was removed, draw two circular lines as though you were stringing together the hearts on both sides. Then, carve a "レ"-shaped groove around this circle.

12

Remove the peel inside the circle so the outline at the hearts are revealed.

13

Carve a rose in the lower left position inside the circle (see p. 164, "big rose").

14

Carve another rose on the right-hand side of the rose carved in step 13. The petals of the two roses should overlap.

15 In the same way, carve another rose on the left-hand side of the rose carved in step 13. The petals of the two roses should also overlap.

16 Trim the area surrounding the roses smooth. Carve a circle with a depth of 1cm outside this circle along the lines in the above picture.

17 Remove the peel between the circle carved in step 16 and the small circle where the hearts are located.

18 This is how it looks after removing the peel and trimming it smooth.

19 Cut slantwise at the position where the peel has been removed in step 18, and carve a smooth "S" shape.

20 Cut slantwise in front of the "S" shape carved in step 19, and shave to make it thinner.

21 Repeat steps 19 and 20 to complete the whole circle. To retain the beauty of the "S" shape, keep its angle and width consistent.

22 Carve "V" shapes under the "S" shapes to make a jagged lace. To make the jagged lace more beautiful, try to maintain the angle, width, and size on both sides.

23 The work is completed when a circle of jagged lace is finished.

wedding

A welcome watermelon

Warmly welcome the wedding guests and express deep gratitude.

| Difficulty | ● ● ● ● ● |

1

7mm
7mm

Place the watermelon on its side and paste a paper stencil on it. Draw a large circle that is based on the illustrated line, and carve two lines spaced 7mm above and below the word.

2

Insert the knife through the paper stencil and carve the letters holding the knife perpendicular to the watermelon. If any letter has a hollow part inside, start carving from the hollow part, and then carve a "レ"-shaped groove on the outer side of the letter. Remove the excess peel from the area surrounding the word enclosed within the top and bottom lines.

182

3

Remove the peel between the top and bottom lines and the circle.

4

The next step is to carve the top and bottom lines into two bow-shaped laces. Carve a "V" groove between the two lines. The distance between two adjacent "V" grooves is 2cm. Smooth "V" shapes are also carved on the circle at equal intervals.

5

Carve each section of the length of 2cm between the two lines into a circle to form the center of a bow. Then, carve a larger circle around this one, forming a ring with a width of 2cm. Then carve a "レ"-shaped groove around the larger circle.

6

Carve the entire circle into an outline consisting of bows.

7

Carve a waterdrop shape on each side of the center of the bow and remove the peel.

8

Repeat step 7 to complete the top and bottom laces of bows.

9

Repeat step 7 to make the entire circle a lace of bows.

10

Cut off the peel below the bow, and carve this part into a smooth "U" shape.

11

Carve an inverted heart shape in the middle of the "U" shape carved in step 10.

183

12

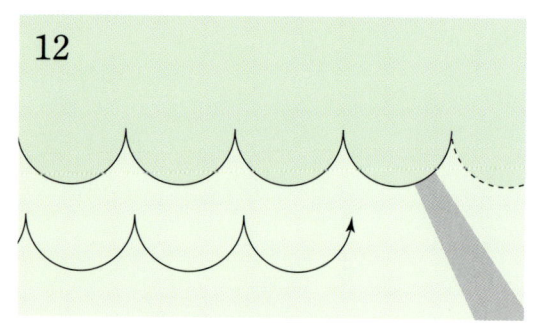

Carve a small wavy line inside of the "U" shape. Move the knife toward the lower right-hand side to carve a semicircle. Then, change the cutting angle slightly to carve the other semicircle. Repeat this process to continuously carve more "U" shapes so that they form a wavy line.

13

Keep the knife horizontal, and carve another wavy line below the one carved in step 12.

14

Repeat steps 12 and 13 on the base surface carved in step 13. Then, continue to carve wavy lines on the outside, and shave the lower part.

15

Carve a rose inside the semicircle below the letters (see p. 164, "big rose").

16

Carve another rose on the right-hand side of the rose carved in step 15. The petals of the two roses should overlap with each other.

17

Fill the semicircle with roses.

18

The interior of the semicircle above the letters is also full of roses.

19

Add a wavy line to the outside of the circle. You can also add other design according to your own preferences based on the overall balance.

wedding

Lettering the couple's names

Roses on a lattice form a striking image.
Add a touch of luxury to this special day!

Difficulty	● ● ● ● ●

1

Place the watermelon on its side and draw two circles based on the illustrated lines. Paste paper stencils between the two circles.

2

Insert the knife through the paper stencil and carve the letters holding the knife perpendicular to the watermelon. If any letter has a hollow part inside, start carving from the hollow part. Then carve a "レ"-shaped groove on the outer side of the letter. Remove the part of the peel between the two circles, except the letters.

3

Based on the illustrated lines, carve grid lines on the part of the peel at the center, with a depth of 2cm. Note that there should be a distance of about 5mm between the grid lines and the edge of the peel.

4

Leave the peel on some of the grid blocks at intervals, and peel the other grid blocks. Then, trim the pulp inside each peeled grid block into a dome shape.

5

Carve a rose on the dome-shaped pulp (see p. 164, "big rose"). Carve four petals in the first layer.

6

Carve three petals in the second layer.

7

Then carve the third and fourth layers with the petals sinking deeper and deeper. A rose is finished.

8

Carve a rose on each grid block of the dome shape in the same way.

9

Carve four eye-like shapes in one of the unpeeled grid blocks.

10

Carve eye-like shapes in all of the unpeeled grid blocks.

11

Carve another circle around this one at a distance of 5mm from the outermost edge.

186

12. Carve a "レ"-shaped groove on the outside of the circle carved in step 11.

13. Carve another circle 4cm below it, and carve a "レ"-shaped groove on the outer side.

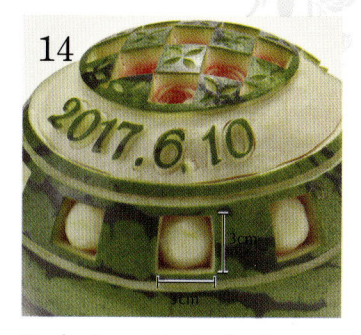

14. On the 4cm-wide circular ring completed in step 13, interlace carved squares with a depth of 2cm and a spacing of 3cm. The pulp exposed inside each square is carved into a dome shape.

15. Repeat steps 5 through 7 to carve all of the dome shapes into roses.

16. Carve four eye-like shapes on the square with peel that lies between two roses.

17. Then, carve eye-like shapes on all of the squares with peel that lie between the roses.

18. Carve a small square pyramid on the circle 5mm from the outer side of the names and date. Then, remove the excess material, and the work is completed.

wedding

Bride silhouette

The silhouette of the bride. Decorate with hearts for added sweetness.

| Difficulty | ●●●●○ |

1 Place the watermelon upright, and paste a paper stencil on it. Draw a large circle that is based on the illustrated line to enclose the silhouette.

2 Insert the knife through the paper stencil and carve the silhouette holding the knife perpendicular to the watermelon. Then, carve a "レ"-shaped groove on the outer side of the outline, and remove all of the peel outside the silhouette and within the circle.

3 Carve a larger circle around the small one, leaving a space of 5mm between the two circles. Carve a "レ"-shaped groove on the outer side of the larger circle.

4 On the outer side of the circle carved in step 3, cut marking lines 1cm deep at intervals of 2cm.

5 On one of the marking lines cut in step 4, carve a line from the upper left-hand side to the lower right-hand side to make the left half.

6 Then, carve another line from the upper right-hand side to the lower left-hand side to join with the line carved in step 5, and form a smooth "V" shape.

7 This is the effect after removing the excess material.

8 Repeat steps 5 and 6 to complete the whole circle.

9 Start carving the heart as shown in the picture. Make a deep cut from the center of the curve to the lower left-hand side, and frame the curve with a line 1cm deep.

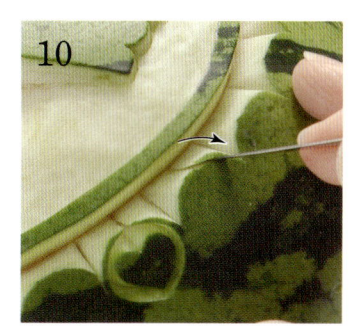

10 Do the same in the opposite direction, by making a deep cut from the center of the curve to the lower right, and frame the curve with a line 1cm deep.

11 Make a cut in the middle downward 1cm deep, which leads directly to the concave dip of the heart.

12 Make a cut from the left-hand side to the center of the heart, and the outline of the upper left-hand-side part of the heart is carved out.

13 Make a cut from the center of the heart to the right-hand side, and the outline of the upper right-hand-side part of the heart is carved out.

14 This is how it looks after removing the excess material produced in the process from steps 9 through 13.

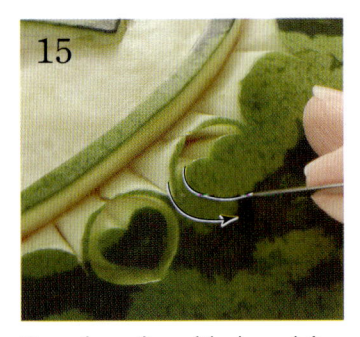

15 Carve the outline of the lower left-hand-side part of the heart with a depth of 1cm.

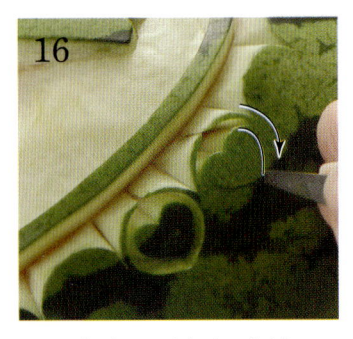

16 Carve the lower right-hand-side part of the heart on the right-hand side with a depth of 1cm.

17 Carve a "レ"-shaped groove on the outer side of the contour line carved in step 15. Pay attention to bringing out a sense of the radian as shown in the picture.

18 This is how it looks after removing the excess material.

19 Repeat the same process on the right-hand side to carve a "レ"-shaped groove on the outer side of the contour line carved in step 16. Bring out a sense of the radian as shown in the picture.

20 This is how it looks after removing the excess material.

21 Carve a "V" shape at the bottom to form the tip of the heart.

190

22 Repeat steps 9 through 21 to complete the whole circle.

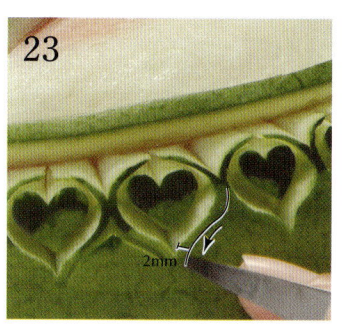

23 Carve a curve 2mm below the surrounding part of the heart to the lower left-hand side.

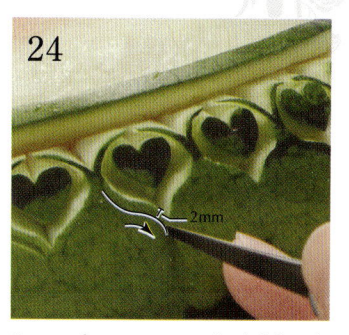

24 Repeat the process on the left-hand side.

25 Carve a "レ"-shaped groove on the outer side of the line carved in step 23.

26 This is how it looks after removing the excess material.

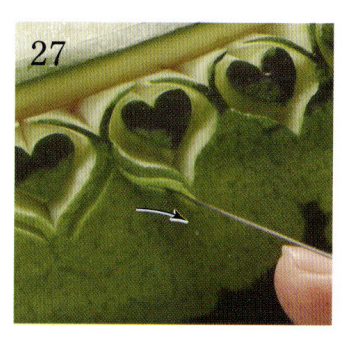

27 Carve a "レ"-shaped groove at the bottom of the line carved in step 24.

28 This is how it looks after removing the excess material.

29 As shown in the picture, carve the outline of an inverted heart between the two sides completed in step 28.

30 On the outer side of the outline carved in step 29, carve a "レ"-shaped groove from the left outer side of the heart.

31 This is how it looks after removing the excess material.

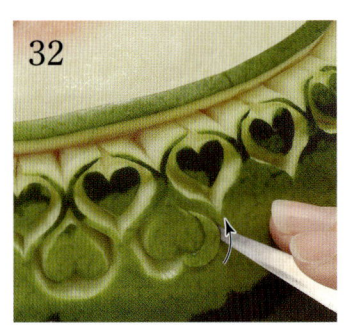

32 On the outer side of the outline carved in step 29, make a "レ"-shaped groove from the right outer side of the heart.

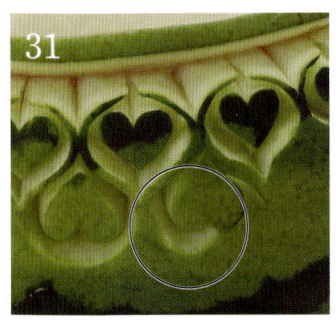

33 This is how it looks after removing the excess material.

34 Trim the lower part to bring out a rounded feel.

35 This is how it looks after removing the excess material.

36 Repeat steps 23 through 35 to complete the whole circle.

37 Outline the trimmed round parts. Carve a circle underneath them. Remove the excess material between the circle and the inverted hearts.

38 Carve a few hearts next to the silhouette, and the work is completed.

193

wedding

Fan theme

An intricate fan-motif, made by carving deeper into the fruit for a beautiful gradation of red.

Difficulty ● ● ● ● ●

1

Place the watermelon on its side, and trace a circle using the lines in the picture as an example. Carve eight equally spaced marks on the outer side of the circle, and connect these marks with curves. The point where the curve is most concave intersects with the circle. Then, cut on these lines, and draw a line with a depth of 1cm.

2

Carve a "レ"-shaped groove on the inner side of the line carved in step 1.

194

3 Remove the peel at the center.

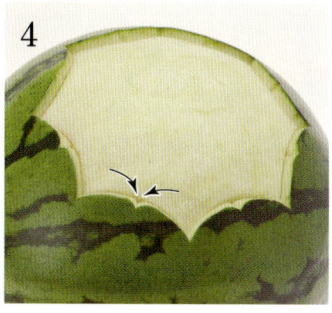

4 Carve a "V" shape at the center of each curve. Follow the order of cutting diagonally from left to right, then from right to left.

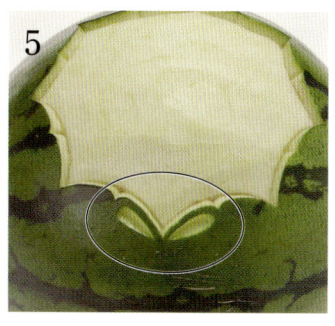

5 Carve two waterdrop shapes in the deep groove on the outer side as shown in the picture, leaving a little bit of peel.

6 Carve another waterdrop below the tips of the two waterdrops.

7 Carve four more waterdrops in the blanks on the left- and right-hand sides.

8 Repeat steps 4 through 7 to complete the whole circle.

9 Carve square pyramids between adjacent shapes. Carve each side slantwise, and remove the excess material from the center. Repeat this process to complete the whole circle.

10 Outline the waterdrop shapes based on the illustrated lines, and carve a circle of lines.

11 Carve "レ"-shaped grooves on the outer side of the lines carved in step 10.

195

12. Trim the part between the shapes completed from step 4 to step 11 smooth. Carve three waterdrop shapes above the trimmed part. Repeat the same process to complete the whole circle.

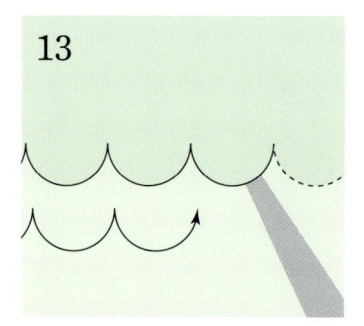

13. Carve small wavy lines on the outer side of the waterdrop shapes. Cut toward the lower right-hand side to carve a semicircle. Then, change the cutting angle slightly to carve the other semicircle. Repeat the same process to continuously carve the fan shapes that surround the waterdrops to form a wavy line.

14. Repeat step 13 to complete a circle of wavy lines.

15. Carve another circle of wavy lines below the wavy lines carved in step 13 by tilting the knife a little more.

16. Carve three waterdrops in the concave section of the waterdrop shapes shown above.

17. Referring to step 13, carve a fan-shaped curve on the outer side of the waterdrops.

18. Tilt the knife and shave the area below the wavy lines carved in step 17. Repeat the same process to complete the whole circle.

19. Referring to step 13, carve another layer of fan-shaped edges on the outside.

20. Tilt the knife and shave the area below the wavy lines carved in step 19. Repeat the same process to complete the whole circle.

21

Carve three waterdrops in the middle part of the shape carved in step 20. Referring to step 13, carve a fan-shaped edge on the outer side the waterdrop. Tilt the knife, and shave the area below the edge line.

22

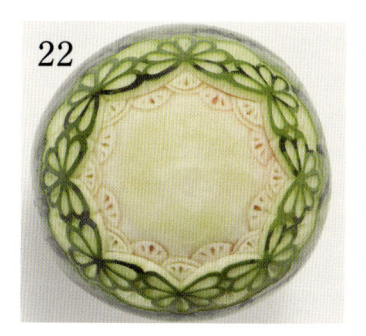

Repeat step 21 to complete the whole circle.

23

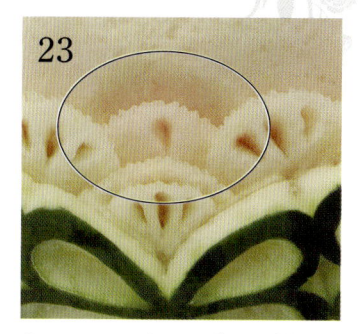

Carve a waterdrop in the middle part of the shape carved in step 22. Referring to step 13, carve a fan-shaped edge on the outer side the waterdrop. Tilt the knife, and shave the area below the edge line.

24

Repeat step 23 to complete the whole circle.

25

Referring to step 13, carve a line of fan shapes in the spaces between the designs completed in step 24. Tilt the knife, and shave the area below the line. Repeat this step to complete the whole circle. To carve deeper into the watermelon, shave the area within the circle until the red fruit becomes slightly visible.

26

Referring to step 13, carve a line of fan shapes in the spaces between the designs completed in step 25. Tilt the knife, and shave the area below the line. Repeat this step to complete the whole circle.

27

This is how it looks from another angle.

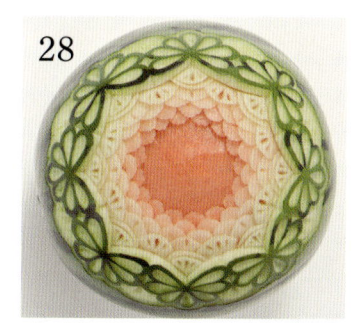

28

Repeat step 26 to complete another circle.

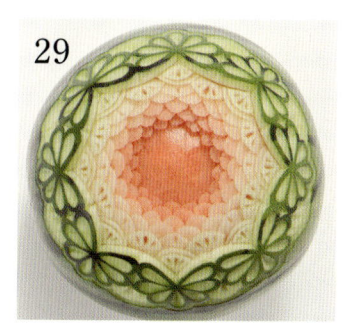

29

Repeat step 26 to continue another circle.

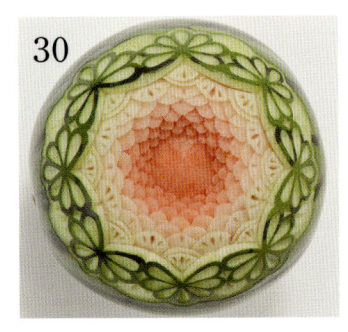

30 Repeat step 26 to complete another circle. The deeper the knife is sunk into the pulp, the smaller the fan shapes.

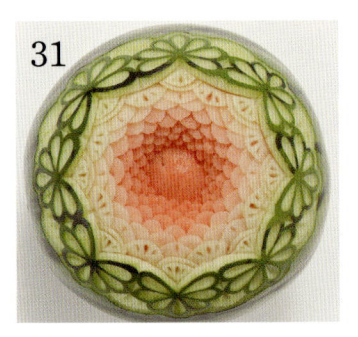

31 Repeat step 26 to complete another circle. Stop carving when the seeds of the watermelon can be seen.

32 This is how it looks from another angle. The internal carving is completed now.

33 Continue to carve patterns on the outside of the watermelon to expand the fan-shaped edges outward. Referring to step 13, carve the fan-shaped edge, and tilt the knife to shave the area below the edge.

34 Repeat step 33 to complete the whole circle.

35 Continue to expand the edge line carved in step 34 outward. Referring to step 13, carve the fan-shaped edge, and tilt the knife to shave the area below the edge.

36 Repeat step 35 to complete the whole circle.

37 This is how it looks from directly above.

Rie and Hitomi's art exhibition

A presentation of their exquisite artwork created with superb craftsmanship and high artistry.

art exhibition

Watermelon pieces

Many people who learn fruit carving aspire to carve a watermelon some day. After struggling with the green peel, the white and red flesh finally become visible. A powerful watermelon piece can taker a viewer's breath away. It is a most gratifying moment, to know that the time and effort involved was not spent in vain.

A welcome watermelon

When welcoming guests, place a welcoming watermelon at the entrance to attract everyone's attention. Note that designs with a lot of the red pulp exposed deteriorate faster. To preserve the work longer, use designs with less red.

Boldly try out a design for the red pulp of a watermelon

Rose motifs are difficult, but it is a shame not to take full advantage of the watermelon's bright red. Try a bold design that cut deep into the fruit, exposing the red pulp. One of the charms of watermelons is that the design does not have to be complex for the work to be stunning.

Free design

It may be difficult to know where to start when carving a watermelon. Carving often begins with a definite design in mind, but sometimes it is best to design as one goes along. It is a great way to experience both the delights and the difficulties of fruit carving.

Repetitive detailed design

Fruit carving is a learned skill, and practice is essential. Designs are usually made from patterns being repeated, and repeating the same size, same shape, same thickness, same depth, requires great concentration and perseverance. These subtle designs are the greatest charm in Hitomi's work.

Combination of your favorite themes

Hitomi's watermelon sculptures combine many hearts, bows and roses. Because a black-skinned watermelon is used here, the lines of the work are very distinct and impressive.

Watermelon bowl in the forest

People often complain that they are too beautiful to eat. Watermelon bowls, however, are made to be eaten, so whenever they appear on the table, everyone is pleased. They make a great gift for a close friend.

art exhibition

Soap carvings

Soap carving is recommended for those who wish to preserve their painstakingly crafted art. As long as they are kept in a cool, dry area, they last a long time and the color does not fade. The scent can also be enjoyed, and it offers a different attraction from fruit carving.

Gift box full of happiness
Send someone a gift box full of flowers carved from soap. The moment the box is opened, joy will be spread everywhere. The techniques acquired in carving can be used in many different places.

Create a luxury jewelry box
Not only does the box contain soap flowers, but the box itself is carved out of soap. The scent is intoxicating, perfect for decorating the entrance hall or living room.

Exquisite and lovely wedding dress
A wedding dress made out of the petals of preserved carnations. The dress is ornamented with soap carved mini carnations.

Use deep carving to show the beauty of shadows
A fine cake carved out of a soap with a diameter of about 7cm. The knife used is the same one used for fruit carving. When using single-colored soap, the design is enhanced by creating deep cuts and shadows.

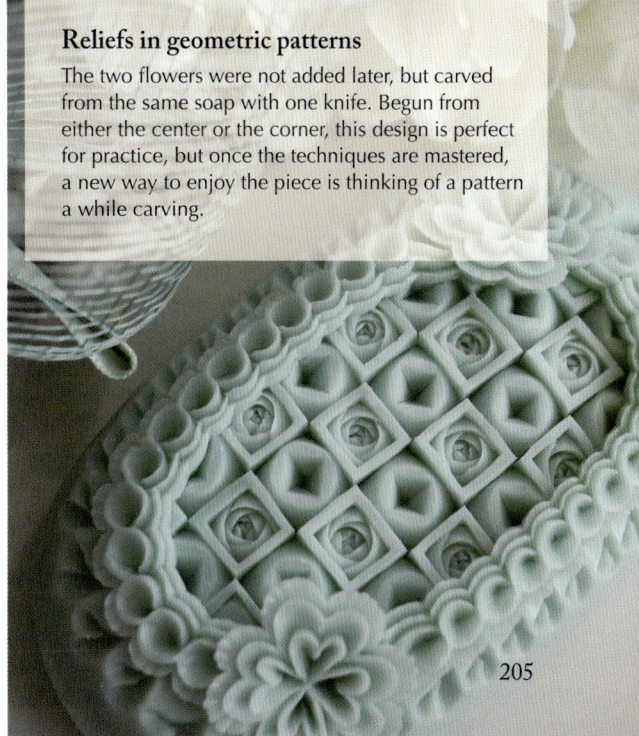

Reliefs in geometric patterns
The two flowers were not added later, but carved from the same soap with one knife. Begun from either the center or the corner, this design is perfect for practice, but once the techniques are mastered, a new way to enjoy the piece is thinking of a pattern a while carving.

Wedding cake
The white flowers around the cake are also carved from soap.

Rie Yamada

Carving Artist. Principal of the carving school "Atelier RIN." She began learning carving techniques and designs in 2004. To increase her skills in method, taste, arrangement and presentation, she studied under various artists not only in Japan, but also in Thailand, the home of fruit carving/the country where fruit carving originated. In 2013, she opened the carving school "Atelier RIN." This book is a collection of her newest designs, all of which are results of her years of research into the changing tastes of carving enthusiasts. Carving has been given increased media exposure over the years, but "Atelier RIN" teaches the beauty and joys of carving which go beyond a temporary trend, contributing to the training of new artists and teachers. Her books include *Enjoying the Four Seasons and Their Festivities: A Textbook of Soap Carving* and *Flower Soap Carving*.

Hitomi Yamada

Carving Artist. Lecturer at "Atelier RIN." She has collaborated with the author on designing and producing the pieces in this book. Her specialty is works of delicate, intricate detail, and she is able to engrave on a piece of soap the size of a palm without diminishing the soft curves of the design. She does not just teach designs at the school, but also teaches the joy of being absorbed in a project, and the sense of accomplishment gained by completing a piece with perseverance and dedication.

Co-producers of the works (Atelier RIN)

Yoshinori Akai	Miyuki Akasabi	Mako Ikeda	Chiaki Iwata
Mai Omura	Kaoru Kakimoto	Yasuko Sakata	Yukari Shigeta
Shizuka Sugiyama	Branislava Setoyama	Aiko Taira	Masato Takayoshi
Shigekazu Tanaka	Izumi Danno	Ryoko Chono	Keiko Terai
Miki Nadai	Tomoko Baba	Megumi Muranishi	

Publisher of Japanese edition: Yuichi Ogawa
Project planning: Rie Yamada
Editing: Emi Kinoshita (ALPHA CREATE Co., LTD.), Manami Matsui (ALPHA CREATE Co., LTD.)
Book design: Emi Kinoshita (ALPHA CREATE Co., LTD.)
Photographs: Shinya Nagano (ALPHA CREATE Co., LTD.), Rie Yamada
Coordination: Mitsuyo Sawada, Rie Yamada
Translation and proofreading: Yang Huiping, Enago English Editing Service, Anna Rhodiner
Thanks to Teruya Nakagawa for help with the photographing
Thanks to Hitomi Yamada for help with the design of work

The Complete Book of Fruit Carving:
Decorate Your Table for Any Special Occasion

English edition published in 2018 by:
NIPPAN IPS Co., Ltd.
1-3-4 Yushima
Bunkyo-ku, Tokyo, 113-0034

ISBN 978-4-86505-145-2

Fruits Carving no Kyokasho
©2017, Rie Yamada.
Original Japanese edition is published by Seibundo Shinkosha Publishing Co., Ltd.

All rights reserved. No part of this book, text, photographs or illustrations may be reproduced or transmitted in any form or by any means by print, photoprint, microfilm, microfiche, photocopier, internet or in any way known or as yet unknown, or stored in a retrieval system, without prior permission in writing from the publisher.

Printed in China